THE EPIC SPLIT

Why 'Made in China' is going out of style
A report from the frontline of the US-China trade war

Johan Nylander

johannylander.asia

One Hour Asia Media Ltd

Editing

Kenny Hodgart

kennyhodgart.co.uk

Cover design

Megan Tanner

thetravellingdesignstudio.com

Cover photos

Inja Pavlic, Lukas Schroder, Marco Bianchetti

unsplash.com

Layout

Liu Hsiu Wen

liuhsiuwen.com

Author photo

Allan Nylander

ISBN: 979-8683662646

MY FREE GIFT TO YOU

If you would like access to a documentary-style presentation
I've made on the topic of this book, please e-mail me at
theepicsplitbook@gmail.com with the subject line FREE GIFT.

This is my way of saying thanks for purchasing this book.

"I've been waiting for somebody to write this book for years. Finally, an authoritative go-to source for the biggest flashpoint of modern times, that of China and the West. The Epic Split is packed full of great insights and anecdotes. It won't leave you feeling comforted, but it will leave you better informed."

— Rob Carnell, Head of Research and Chief Economist,
Asia-Pacific, ING Bank (Singapore)

"The Epic Split is a fascinating read. It offers a frontliner's account of a tectonic shift in global politics and business. Essential reading."

— Risto E J Penttilä, Secretary General,
European Business Leaders' Convention (Helsinki)

"It was a pure pleasure reading his book. Highly relevant – and elegant."

— Ulf Ohrling, Founder and Director,
Ohrling Advisory Ltd (Hong Kong)

"Johan Nylander offers a balanced look at the deep set of problems facing US-China relations, and is particularly trenchant in laying the difficulties companies will face in choosing sides in this titanic struggle.

"Nylander does a superb job of unpacking the state of decoupling between US and China, and outlining the trajectory of both economic, but also technology-related decoupling, highlighting that this will be a lengthy and messy process.

— *Paul Triolo, Head of Geo-technology at Eurasia Group, and Senior Advisor at the Paulson Institute (New York)*

"What happens when the top two economic powers in the world are at loggerheads? Read this concise, and highly entertaining, book to find out."

— *Louis-Vincent Gave, Co-founder and CEO, Gavekal Research (Hong Kong)*

INTRODUCTION

This book is about the greatest break-up the world has ever seen.

The conflict between the world's two biggest economies is far from being just about trade. It's a fierce and escalating battle between two ideologies. If the past decades were characterized by globalization, the next may well be all about decoupling: the disintegration of the relationship between the US and China.

Companies are leaving China, no question. And consumers around the world say they prefer products not made there. It's clear that 'Made in China' is going out of fashion.

However, this is not a book about the world going up in flames. It's about change and opportunities. For China, the conflict has given new urgency to the need to modernize its economy and become more self-reliant in technology. For international companies and for governments around the world, it has been a wake-up call to cut dependency on Chinese supply chains, against a backdrop of rising consumer skepticism toward China. The world's biggest maker of mobile phones, Samsung Electronics, recently closed down its last factory in China. More will follow.

It doesn't really matter whether Donald Trump, Joe Biden or someone else sits in the White House. This conflict – this epic split – runs deeper, and will continue to dominate the global political and trade landscape for many years to come. The fight has just begun.

"As de-globalization accelerates, two hostile economic blocs are emerging, one centered around China and the other around the United States," Harvard researcher Michael Witt has said. The Chairman of Foxconn, the maker of Apple's iPhone, believes "China's days as the world's factory are done." What happens next? When I spoke with democracy activist Joshua Wong here in Hong Kong, he declared with determination that "Actions speak louder than words."

It's incredible how much has happened since I published my last book, 2017's 'Shenzhen Superstars – How China's smartest city is challenging Silicon Valley'. Back then there was a general curiosity about China Inc. People wanted to understand how in just a few decades the country had become a high-tech and innovation powerhouse. International delegations were flooding into Shenzhen, and my book became an Amazon bestseller. I found myself traveling across Asia and Europe to give speeches – to organizations as diverse as JP Morgan, Calvin Klein, the American and European Chambers of Commerce and the Asia Society – on how China's tech startups were catching up with or even overtaking Western rivals, and the challenges this created in terms of business competitiveness and democratic values.

In the intervening years, the sentiment toward China has turned from curiosity to suspicion. When organizations ask me to give speeches today it's typically about how to navigate and find opportunities in a new and evolving world of trade aggression, decoupling and consumer boycotts.

As a journalist based in Hong Kong for the last decade, I have enjoyed a ring-side view of the astonishing transformation in trade and diplomatic relations between China and the West. Political actions taken in Hong Kong, by the government and its opponents alike, can be seen as a portent of a Beijing-led world. I don't know how many times I've stood in a cloud of teargas, amid demonstrators fighting for democratic values on one side and police enforcing authoritarian rule on the other. Some welcome Hong Kong being integrated more deeply into mainland China and the policies of the Communist regime. Others fight it. The city has also found itself in the crossfire between Washington and Beijing. As the global conflict deepens, I often feel more like a trade war correspondent than an Asia correspondent. I'm aware of pacing the faultlines of this new battle of ideologies, in a place where history is unfolding as I write.

Happy reading.

P.S. It should go without saying, but let me underscore something. Criticisms of China in this book, by many interviewees and by myself, are leveled at the government, not at the country and its people more generally. It follows the same logic that you don't have to be anti-American just because you criticize Trump or Biden, or anti-Swedish just because you don't like IKEA or ABBA.

TIME FOR SOME DECISIONS

Before we kick off, let me offer a little thought experiment. It actually connects back to the title of the book.

Do you remember the action movie star Jean-Claude Van Damme doing his "epic split" between two moving trucks in a commercial for Volvo some years back? He has one foot on each truck's side mirror as the two vehicles slowly back up and move further apart.

Now, imagine one truck is the US and the other China, and you are Van Damme. As the trucks pull away from one another, you will have to decide which truck – which party in the trade war – to side with.

While you're making up your mind, the driver of the American truck is adding allies on its trailer, countries like the UK, Australia and Japan, and speaking of democracy and freedoms. On the other side, the Chinese driver distracts you with talk of booming consumer demand, AI supremacy and Belt and Road riches. The only thing that you know for sure is that you can't stay where you are for long, no matter how good you are at doing the splits. At some point soon, you will have to make your decision.

ABOUT THE AUTHOR

Johan Nylander is an award-winning author and freelance China and Asia correspondent. His work is published by CNN, Forbes, Sweden's leading business daily Dagens Industri, and many other international media outlets.

Nylander has covered news from a wide range of countries outside of his native Sweden for almost two decades. Today – at least when there are no travel restrictions – he spends most of his time roaming around China and neighboring countries, conducting interviews with the people who will shape the Asia of tomorrow: presidents and peasants, entrepreneurs and migrant workers, triad members and government officials.

He is the author of 'Shenzhen Superstars – How China's smartest city is challenging Silicon Valley', which became an Amazon bestseller. He is also a co-writer of 'Shenzhen: China's Southern Powerhouse', a coffee table-sized book of photos published by Odyssey Books, and the author of an acclaimed management book called 'Simplify' (Förenkla!, Liber publishing).

During the 2008 financial crisis, Nylander was stationed as a foreign correspondent in London. He has an MBA from the University of Gothenburg.

Nylander lives with his family in Hong Kong.

For more about him, and to stay informed about his next book, visit johannylander.asia.

TABLE OF CONTENT

Make it or break it *1*

Top dog again *15*

Dangerous dynamics *29*

The great sellout *35*

Emptying the cage *41*

High-tech pullout *49*

Year in a word: Decoupling *59*

The Splinternet *71*

One company, two systems *79*

Financial Iron curtain *93*

Chokehold on drugs *99*

China's Long March to self-reliance *107*

Lessons on resistance *119*

Boycott as political weapon *129*

Bonus chapter – 'Shenzhen Superstars' abstract *152*

Acknowledgements *162*

MAKE IT OR BREAK IT

"We're in an economic war with China"

One day, while walking in Beijing, American diplomat Charlene Barshefsky heard a man call her name. She stopped – and saw a family of three approaching her.

"I turned around, and it was this gentleman, and he thanked me for the WTO, which of course made me laugh, because most people in the United States would have no idea what the WTO is," Barshefsky told the China Daily newspaper in an interview.

"He simply wanted me to know that his son would have a better life. This was completely overwhelming to me. Obviously, he equated WTO entry with personal development, with that rise as part of this process for China."

When Chinese state-controlled media portray Charlene Barshefsky, the former United States Trade Representative who paved the way for China's entry to the world's biggest trading bloc – the World Trade Organization – in 2001, it's typically by way of oily anecdotes like the one above, affirming China's commitments to open trade and globalization.

The China Daily interview continues by explaining how Barshefsky – today a senior partner at WilmerHale, a Washington-based law firm – looks back with "great pride" on her role in helping China achieve WTO membership after 15 years of trying, that she has been "extremely positive" for the country and the world, and that she has never regretted her support.

"Could there be any doubt that China should be in the WTO? Of course not," she is quoted as saying. "I'm often asked, 'Was it a mistake?' And I'm answering you unequivocally: No. It was not a mistake; it was an extremely positive move for China and for the world."

When Barshefsky took to the stage in Hong Kong, in October 2019, at a high-level conference organized by the city's American Chamber of Commerce and attended by some of Asia's top business leaders – as well as former and current advisors to Barack Obama and Donald Trump – she painted rather a different picture, however.

It was not a mistake to let China join the WTO, she said. It was a mistake, though, not to have mechanisms to ensure China followed the rules.

During her presentation, she did not hide her disappointment at the leaders in Beijing, calling China's protectionism "the single biggest threat to the global system". Nor did she hide her frustration with the Trump administration for walking down a similarly dangerous path of protectionism and discriminatory practices.

"The question is: Will we let the global trade and investment system, that has created extraordinary global growth and stability, fall into disrepair and eventually collapse – or will we go forward and revitalize it?" she asked, looking down at her audience over thin reading glasses, like a stern school-teacher. "The world's two largest trading nations, the United States and China, are disproportionately responsible for answering this question."

The WTO is to global trade what oil is to an engine. When iPhones move from China to America, or bottles of Bordeaux wine from the European Union to Japan, it is the WTO's rules that keep tariff and non-tariff barriers low and give companies the certainty they need to plan and invest. It underpins 96 percent of global trade, according to The Economist. By one estimate, membership of the WTO, or its predecessor, the General Agreement on Tariffs and Trade (GATT), has boosted trade among members by 171 percent.

Let's roll back the tape a bit. After years of negotiation between the US and China during the 1990s, Barshefsky addressed the US Congress during a committee hearing titled 'Accession of China to the WTO' on May 3, 2000. Chairman Bill Archer introduced her as "a lady that has done yeoman work in negotiating trade agreements on behalf of this country".

Beaming with hope, Barshefsky told the committee the agreement with China would give access to "a market that will be the largest single market in the world" and offer opportunities for exporters of industrial goods, farm products and services "to a degree unprecedented in the modern era".

It would strengthen America's ability to enforce China's trade commitments and normalize trade relations between the countries. It would enable foreign companies to "participate in information industries such as telecommunications, including the Internet". It would address China's practice of technology transfer as a condition of investment. China Inc would become more market-oriented, less state-controlled.

In short: "[China's admission] will strengthen our guarantees of fair trade."

Joining the WTO would, moreover, advance China towards deploying Western-style rule of law, spur progress toward democratization and end the Communist party's systematic human rights violations. She even cited endorsements from Martin Lee, one of Hong Kong's most prominent campaigners for democracy and human rights, and Bao Tong, a former party official who served a seven-year jail term in the wake of the 1989 military crackdown on the Tiananmen Square movement.

Barshefsky continued: "[The commitments] will give China's people more access to information, and weaken the ability of hardliners in government to isolate China's public from outside influences and ideas.

"More deeply, they reflect a judgment that prosperity, security and international respect will not come from the static nationalism, state power and state control over the economy China adopted after the war, but that China's own interests are best served by the advancing economic freedom, engagement with the world, and ultimately development of the rule of law inherent in the initiative President Truman began in 1948 with the founding of the GATT."

As had also been spelt out by the country's then president, Bill Clinton, in a speech he made in 2000, the thinking in America was that as the barriers protecting China's state-owned industries were lowered, Beijing could be expected to speed up its departure from a state-led economic system, which Clinton identified as being a major source of the Communist Party's power.

The following year – on 11 December, 2001 – China was finally able to bask in its welcome to the club. The first steps toward a more mutually prosperous, safe and globalized world had been taken. There was hope in the air, like a fresh breeze on a spring morning, and it could be felt in both Washington and Beijing.

Now, almost two decades later, most pundits call bullshit on the deal.

In her speech in Hong Kong, Charlene Barshefsky said that expectations were initially high that Beijing would honor its commitments and gradually depart from its party-controlled economic and political structures. Those hopes dimmed as early as 2006, however. After that, she said, Beijing turned its back on robust market changes and adopted a "significantly state-run" model that discriminates against foreign companies. This trend has not slowed down since – quite the opposite.

"From Deng [Xiaoping, the architect of China's radical opening up reforms in the late 1970s] to 2006, or so, China had been on a more convergent course with market-based economies," Barshefsky told the AmCham. "But, beginning around 2006 or 2007, the reform and opening which had characterized the previous 20 years began to sputter. Policies such as 'indigenous innovation' were inaugurated. By the time Xi Jinping came into office, reform and opening had virtually halted. Indeed, even while Hu Jintao was president, the words 'reform' and 'opening' were rarely coupled together, and the word 'opening' began to drop out entirely."

Scroll forward a decade and barely a day passes without reports of how international companies doing business in China must contend with forced transfers of technology, theft of intellectual property, discrimination or lack of market access. In a 2019 study by the American Chamber of Commerce in China, 75 percent of polled member companies, the highest ever, said they felt they were less welcome in China than previously. The chamber called the data "astounding".

Reports by the EU Chamber of Commerce in China show similar sentiment among European business leaders. Almost half of European respondents in a 2020 poll said the business environment in China had become more political and that they felt "sometimes under threat of punishment by authorities". Almost half of respondents said market access barriers were a problem, and that doing business in China had become more difficult over the past year. They also expressed increased concern that state-controlled enterprises in China would gain opportunities at the expense of the private sector.

As a marker of the failure, almost two decades along the road, to properly assimilate China into WTO procedures, AmCham still hopes Washington will push more strongly for a level playing field for American businesses in China. Their persistence is almost charmingly credulous.

It is perhaps worth recalling at this juncture that when China originally applied for membership to the GATT, in 1986, negotiations were interrupted not only by the Tiananmen Square Massacre, in 1989, but also by "disagreements over market access, intellectual property rights, and other matters", according to a 1999 report by the National Bureau of Asian Research, a think tank. Sound familiar?

Today, Charlene Barshefsky not only slams Beijing's deviation from market principles but also inaction by other WTO members, including previous US administrations, for helping to cause the current standoff.

Not that the Trump administration gets off the hook, either. Barshefsky warned in a 2019 Bloomberg interview that the dumbest approach to stopping China from exploiting the free trade rules of the WTO would be to try to copy its protectionist policies and industrial planning. As we have all come to know, increased protectionism has been a cornerstone of Trump's "America first" policies.

"We'll never out-China China," Barshefsky said. "And if you spent 10 minutes in the country, you'd know that."

Her comments echo the gloomy notes struck by a succession of other high-profile speakers at the American Chamber of Commerce in Hong Kong's China Conference.

Max Baucus, a former US Ambassador to Beijing, said that China and the United States are locked in a "kind of cold war" that is more difficult to resolve than the four-decade stand-off between the US and the Soviet Union. The Soviets thought they could crush the capitalist system, whereas the Chinese depend on it. He said that the root of the US-China dispute is that "we do not trust each other" and warned that "It's very dangerous. I personally think we're sliding toward a longer term dispute than many people imagined was possible."

Evan Medeiros, senior director for Asia on the US National Security Council during the Obama administration, said that the world has entered "a new normal that is defined by a period of persistent and consistent tensions".

"Many American strategists recognize we're now dealing with a rising power, that our interests diverge more than they converge and they diverge on important American economic and security interests," Medeiros said at the conference. "It's a similar calculation on China's part."

It should be noted that the diplomats just quoted are fairly moderate in their views - and that their comments came before the outbreak of the covid-19 virus, which has further undermined global trust. These individuals are not your typical China hawks. Despite deep political divides in the United States, there exists increasingly broad support in Washington and around the country for holding China to account for its behavior, including unfair trade practices and cyber theft.

• A July 2020 survey from the Pew Research Center showed anti-China sentiment in the US to be at an historic high. The polling found that 73 percent of Americans have an unfavorable view of China, the highest level since Pew started asking the question 15 years ago.

• More than a quarter of Americans now classify China as an enemy of the United States, according to the same survey. That's almost double the level since the question was last asked, in 2012.

• Faith in President Xi Jinping has also deteriorated, with 77 percent of Americans saying they have little or no faith in him to do the right thing in global affairs.

• A recent Harvard CAPS-Harris Poll survey found that 53 percent of American voters view China as an enemy, and 70 percent say the country is responsible for creating new global tensions.

• A 2020 survey by the British-based Institute for Global Change research group found that 60 percent of British and French citizens now view Beijing as a "force for bad" in the world. Only 3 percent of Britons, 4 percent of Germans and 5 percent of French and American respondents identified China as a "force for good".

• Global views of China are mixed, according to a 2019 Pew study. Opinion varies considerably, from a high of 71 percent with favorable views in Russia to a low of 14 percent in Japan.

• In Japan, 75 percent said Chinese investments are bad. In Nigeria, only 14 percent disapproved of investments from China.

Meanwhile, harsh words traverse the globe in both directions.

Donald Trump has blamed China for covering up the coronavirus pandemic he has repeatedly branded "Kung Flu", accused Beijing of "illicit espionage to steal our industrial secrets" and threatened that the US could pursue a "complete decoupling" from the country.

Likewise, presidential candidate Joe Biden has described President Xi as a "thug", labeled the mass detention of Uighur Muslims unconscionable and accused China of predatory trade practices.

For their part, China's leaders and state-controlled media have described American politicians in terms ranging from "shameless" to "evil". They have even branded Trump a "big-mouthed clown".

That's hardly the refined diplomatic language we were previously accustomed to.

Even with a change of administration in the White House, the situation will likely remain tense and relations edgy, according to many with skin in the game.

Last year I conducted an interview with Ren Zhengfei, founder of the Chinese telecom giant Huawei. He told me it doesn't matter to his business who is president of the United States. "No one in the US will speak for Huawei," he said. "The US may or may not elect a new president, but this will not change their policy towards us. We must be mentally prepared for this for a long time to come." (More about Huawei and Ren later.)

Let's also consider the view of Steve Bannon, a former adviser to Trump and co-founder of a think tank named 'Committee on the Present Danger: China'. Whatever you might think of Bannon, he still pulls weight in Washington and other capitals where dissatisfaction with the world order and populist politics have taken root. Here's what he has had to say:

"China's model for the past 25 years, it's based on investment and exports. Who financed that? The American working class and middle class." (New York Times)

"The CCP has chosen to exploit the free and open rules-based order and attempt to reshape the international system in its favor." (The Wire China)

"We're in an economic war with China. It's futile to compromise." (Washington Post)

Unsurprisingly, Bannon and many other American politicians, Democrat and Republican alike, believe China has abused the WTO to gain unfair advantage over the US.

What's clear is that the WTO is an organization in crisis and that it's failing to align the interests of China and the US. In a recent interview, Sweden's foreign trade minister, Anna Hallberg, told me the WTO faces a "make it or break it" situation. Without great reforms, she said, it might lose its significance and its reasons to exist.

Henry Gao, Associate Professor of Law at Singapore Management University, takes the argument even further, arguing that the WTO needs a new set of rules to confront the challenges brought by China's unique economic system, with its heavy reliance on state-owned enterprises (SOEs) and government subsidies. From his perspective, the existing WTO rulebook is inadequate for dealing with China.

So why keep referring to the WTO? Because while it remains the most important symbol of organized global free trade, it's collapsing under the strains of this escalating conflict between its two most powerful members. Together, the US and China account for 40 percent of the world's gross domestic product. China is the world's biggest exporter, while the US is its biggest importer. Ripple effects from such a trade dispute are naturally massive and not to be taken lightly.

A likely scenario, as I see it, is that the influence of the WTO will continue to diminish, with governments drawing up their own agendas and making their own judgments as to what's "fair" trade and what isn't. And that might in turn lead to greater geopolitical turbulence – and to further deglobalization, decoupling and boycotts.

Oh, and one more thing. Adding to present difficulties is that the WTO system is meant to be self-reinforcing. There's no 'sheriff'. Well, good luck with that.

TOP DOG AGAIN

"One-party autocracy [...] can also have great advantages"

The case against China has been well-rehearsed. But is it fair to blame only one side for the conflict? Of course not.

In many ways, it's understandable that China doesn't want to be forced into a Western-style political and economic system, and it has actually been quite clear about that all along. As an acquaintance of mine, an American lawyer who previously worked for the United Nations, put it to me: China is the first emerging economy with the muscle not to have to bow to the US. China is strong and confident enough to choose its own path, just as it has over the centuries.

During the negotiations to join the WTO, China's then president, Jiang Zemin, came under attack from nationalistic opposition leaders for "selling out the country" and being soft on the United States. Student demonstrators in May 1999 labeled him a "traitor". Other critics blasted "globalization" as a mask for Americanization, and in a way they had a point. The international dollar-dominated trade system was, and still is, based on Western ideals of what's fair and what's not. Even with the best of intentions, it should not come as a surprise that Beijing has proved hesitant about fully embracing such a system and giving up its own ideas about politics and society.

China's leaders have a great belief in a state-capitalist model. The "China model" has become shorthand for economic liberalization without political liberalization. It has made China rich, not democratic. Speaking with people in China – from the business elites to your average person on the street – many (not all) agree that the heavy hand of Beijing is a necessity for social stability. I don't know how many times I've heard people say that democracy in China would lead to chaos. According to the Edelman Trust Barometer, people in China have more trust in their own country's institutions – chiefly their government – than anyone anywhere else in the world.

In hindsight, the signs of Beijing's rejection of a Western democratic and capitalistic model have always been obvious. In January 2009, premier Wen Jiabao stepped up on the stage at the World Economic Forum in Davos – the first Chinese communist party politician to attend the meeting – and gave the audience the lecture of a lifetime. The global financial crises were in full rage, and Wen bluntly put the blame on the Western leaders and a capitalist system based on greed. An "excessive expansion of financial institutions in blind pursuit of profit", a failure of government supervision of the financial sector, and an "unsustainable model of development, characterized by prolonged low savings and high consumption" had caused the crisis, Wen said. The Chinese premier did not hold back his resentment.

That year China's economy grew by nearly 9 percent, while Japan's shrank by over 5 percent, and the American economy contracted by 2.6 percent. It was China that helped kick-start a global recovery after the financial crisis with a half-a-trillion-dollar spending splurge. Obviously, they were doing something right – and got a lot of praise for it too, sometimes from the most unexpected camps.

"One-party autocracy certainly has its drawbacks. But when it is led by a reasonably enlightened group of people, as in China today, it can also have great advantages," wrote the influential New York Times columnist Thomas Friedman, in 2009. "One party can just impose the politically difficult but critically important policies needed to move a society forward."

Over my years covering China and travelling in the country, I have met numerous Western business people with a sweet tooth for its authoritarian system. Let me share a short anecdote.

Some years ago I was having drinks with a friend at an outdoor bar in Guangzhou when a middle-aged man from Germany at the table next to ours sparked a conversation with us about politics. He didn't have much to say in favor of European liberal values. Being in the business of selling fish tanks and other fish hobby equipment – I remember him as the Fish Tank Man – and taking regular business trips to China, he had picked up an affection for its undemocratic model.

"Europe is dying," he stressed. "Everything is too slow. If you want to build a motorway in Germany it takes decades. You have to listen to every single tree-hugger who stands in the way. Here in China it's more efficient. If there's a village in the way of the planned motorway," he said, sweeping with his hand over the table, "the government removes the villagers. No problem."

To this picture of Chinese efficiency, let's add the undeniable fact that it has been the world's biggest economy for much of the last 2,000 years – and was so up until about 200 years ago. According to a study by the economist Angus Maddison, China accounted for an estimated 33 percent of global GDP in 1820. And following a century and a half of turmoil, it has made a jaw-dropping comeback over the last 40 years – from chaos and mass-starvation under Mao Zedong to its current position as a global economic and innovation powerhouse.

In 2010, China replaced Japan as the world's second-largest economy, and many economists believe it is only a matter of time before it dethrones the United States as the world's biggest; some have argued that could happen before 2030. In purchasing power parity (PPP) terms, China is already number one.

As many Chinese see it, the last two centuries were just a brief moment in history of non-supremacy.

Look at China today. Whatever you care to measure, in terms of business and wealth creation, the country is doing pretty well. I'll just highlight the most obvious indicators:

• In 1980, China's economy was smaller than that of the Netherlands. Today, the yearly increments of growth in China's GDP alone are greater than the entire Dutch economy.

• China has more companies on the Fortune Global 500 list than the US. Of these, 80 percent are state-controlled enterprises.

• China has the world's second-highest number of billionaires, but the most people among the world's richest 10 percent.

• China is the larest single creditor in the world, and the second largest holder of US government debt (with about US$1.1 trillion worth of US Treasury bonds in its foreign reserves).

In non-economic terms China has much to be proud of, too. For example: A child born in Beijing today has a longer official life expectancy than a child born in Washington or New York City. Extreme poverty has been next to eradicated, and kids in Chinese cities like Shanghai regularly score higher than Western kids in global education and intelligence rankings.

A 2017 international study of Generation Z concluded that young people in China have a more positive view of the future than any of their counterparts around the world. And, interestingly, the same poll also suggested Chinese young people were the least convinced among their peers elsewhere of the value of international cooperation. Only 10 percent thought more cooperation between nations would solve global challenges, according to the study by the Varkey Foundation, a British NGO. Meanwhile, even if people in Western counties have an increasingly unfavorable view of China and see the country as an enemy, as explained earlier, those in emerging markets have a relatively more positive view of the Asian giant, according to a Pew Research Center survey.

So when Xi Jinping looks out at the world, he can do so with confidence. He bows to no one. China is back where it belongs, as top dog.

Or, as The Economist explained: Officials and scholars in Beijing no longer bother to conceal their impatience and scorn for an America they view – with a perilous mix of hubris and paranoia – as old, tired and clumsy.

"In China's telling, American companies became accustomed to making fat profits in China, but see Chinese rivals catching them up and potentially setting global standards for future technologies. Now American businesses are crying cheat, and demanding that trade rules designed for the rich world be used to keep China down," it said.

"Chinese officials say that America failed to educate workers, allowd inequalities to yawn and never built social safety-nets to help victims of globalization – and is now scapegoating China for those ills."

It is clear, I would suggest, that hopes of China following the paths of Japan and Germany – and taking its place as a responsible and obedient stakeholder in the international order that America has built over the past seven decades – have died.

I don't know how many times I've heard Chinese politicians, spokespersons, think tanks and state-controlled media repeat the same promises of reforms to open up markets and create a fair business environment. The European Union's mission in Beijing even warned of "promise fatigue".

Almost 20 years after joining the WTO, the International Monetary Fund (IMF) still repeatedly urges China to adopt further steps to open its market, and has disputed Beijing's assessment of the country's progress in reforming state-owned enterprises and reducing trade and investment restrictions.

"The Chinese economy is still very restrictive," said Alfred Schipke, the IMF's chief China representative, at a symposium in Beijing in 2018.

Despite having gradually opened to foreign trade and

investment, China remains less open than other G20 emerging market economies in services and foreign direct investment, the organization believes.

Many experts were similarly skeptical when Beijing and Washington signed their so-called phase-one trade agreement in early 2020. The deal not only required the Chinese to purchase more American agricultural products, energy and manufactured goods and to address complaints about intellectual property practices and forced technology transfers, it also prepared the way for another phase of negotiations and actions aimed at creating a more market-oriented playing field in China.

However the ink had barely dried on the paper the deal was signed on before president Xi approved a plan to *enhance* the role of state-owned enterprises in China's economy. That approval, experts said, sent a clear message that China's ruling Communist Party has no plans to drop its support for the state sector, despite long-standing complaints from the United States, the European Union and Japan about unfair treatment of privately-owned multinationals. Eurasia Group, an analyst house, called the phase-one agreement a "zombie deal".

Although private firms are the main engine of China's profit-making and innovation, its state-controlled giants have a massive influence on both the Chinese and the international economies. Those state-owned companies – which dominate industries as disparate as banking, telecommunications and resources – account for around 30 percent of China's economy and contribute to the government's tight control over all aspects of economic and social life in the country. As mentioned before, some 80 percent of Chinese companies on the Fortune Global 500 list are state-controlled enterprises.

It's unlikely that Beijing will ever give up its loyal titans.

"Beijing has developed a hybrid form of capitalism in which it has opened its economy to some extent, but it also ensures the government controls strategic industries, picks corporate winners, determines investments by state funds, and pushes the banking sector to support national champion firms," Joshua Kurlantzick, senior fellow for Southeast Asia at the Council on Foreign Relations, wrote in an opinion piece.

"China – and to a lesser extent other successful authoritarian capitalists – offer a viable alternative to the leading democracies. In many ways, their systems pose the most serious challenge to democratic capitalism since the rise of communism and fascism in the 1920s and early 1930s."

Members of the EU Chamber of Commerce in China have argued that competing in a state-dominated sector is increasingly difficult, even adding that "China is moving toward a 'one economy, two systems' model."

In a special report, The Economist looked at the rise of China's new state capitalism and suggested Xi Jinping is not simply inflating the state at the expense of the private sector. Rather, he is presiding over what he hopes will be the creation of a more muscular form of state capitalism. The idea, the magazine said, is for state-owned companies to gain from more market discipline and for private enterprises to gain from party discipline, all the better to achieve China's great collective mission.

"It is getting harder to distinguish between the state and private sectors. It is getting harder to distinguish between corporate and national interests," the report stated. It then added, perhaps to chagrin of some China hawks, that: "For all its inefficiencies, contradictions and authoritarianism, not to mention its increasingly pious cult of personality, it is getting harder to claim that state capitalism will hobble China's attempts to produce companies and master technologies that put it on the world economy's leading edge."

The "Chinese Dream", as formulated by Xi, is a collective dream for China to become rich and powerful as one. In that sense, it's opposed to the "American Dream", which is focused on the individual and on individual success.

Meanwhile, Party committees have mushroomed in private enterprises, and have become more influential in business decision-making. Private Chinese companies are today increasingly open about their links to the Communist Party. By The Economist's count, nearly 400 of the 3,900 companies listed on stock exchanges in mainland China paid homage to the Communist Party and its leader in their annual reports in 2020. These numbers are likely to rise.

When Western politicians say China's leaders are lying about its political ambitions, that's not quite true. Xi has been clear. In 2013, he vowed that China would "let the market play the decisive role in allocating resources" – but also reinforce "the leading role of the state-owned sector".

Here are more quotes from some of Xi's many and long speeches:

"The goal to push forward reform lays on the constant self-improvement and development of the socialist system, to invest vigor and vitality to the socialist system. Here the core is to uphold and improve the leadership by the Party, to uphold and perfect the socialist system with Chinese characteristics, and it would be poles apart if we stray from this path."

"We must, unswervingly, reinforce the development of the state economy while, unswervingly, encouraging, supporting and guiding the development of the non-state economy."

"We have to beware not to fall into the snare of division or Westernization."

Critics within the party have repeatedly warned that Xi is pushing his agenda too far, and not just alienating foreign friends and trade partners but breaking down the structure of his own party and political system. He has scrapped any time limit on the presidency, effectively making himself "Emperor for life", and has built a Mao-style cult of personality around himself. Almost a decade in, rule by fear is well-established as Xi's core method – both inside and outside of the party.

Cai Xia, a former professor at China's elite Central Party School, recently accused Xi of "killing a country" and said that many party members now want to get out. In an interview with The Guardian in August 2020, she said the president's "unchecked power" has made China "the enemy of the world." She claimed discontent within the party is widespread.

"Under the regime of Xi, the Chinese Communist party is not a force for progress for China. In fact, it is an obstacle to China's progress," she added.

"It is a vicious cycle. After a wrong decision is made, the result is not good. But those below are too afraid to tell him and wrong decisions continue to be made until the situation is out of control. In this vicious cycle, there is no way to stop the country from sliding towards disaster."

She also said that the growing tension between the US and China is a "confrontation between the free, democratic system versus the CCP's new form of authoritarianism".

Over the last months, and at the time of writing, China has seemed determined to wage conflict on multiple fronts. It has ordered the closure of a US consulate in response to a similar move from the US; fought a deadly border clash with India; heralded an abrupt end to a so-called "golden era" of relations with the UK; engaged in a war of words with Australia, sinking relations with Canberra close to an all-time low; implemented a national security law in Hong Kong, earning international condemnation; and fallen further into a rivalry with the US that is forcing other countries to choose sides. Increasingly, they are choosing the US. Meanwhile, the jabs keep flying between Washington and Beijing.

For Chinese citizens, whether party cadres, business leaders, high-tech professionals or factory workers, and whether loyal to the regime or not, these growing international conflicts must surely be a wakeup call that things are not as they were.

For the last 40 years, China has lived a largely peaceful existence, but there is a sense of that having changed. Having stoked tensions, its top leader is not about to back down. Indeed, in a meeting with American, European and Australian business leaders in Beijing in the early days of the trade war, Xi – according to the Wall Street Journal – promised a bare-knuckle approach in countering Trump's trade aggressions.

"In the West, you have a notion that if somebody hits you on the left cheek, you turn the other cheek," Xi reportedly said. "In our culture, we punch back."

DANGEROUS DYNAMICS

"China wants to be China and accepted as such – not as an honorary member of the West"

During a speech I recently gave about the trade conflict and decoupling, a woman from China asked me a straight-up question: "Is there a risk that the conflict between Washington and Beijing ultimately could go from a 'cold war' to a 'hot war?'"

The question is valid. In the Pacific, military muscles are being flexed and geopolitical tensions heightened. Reading both American and Chinese media, and talking with friends and experts, it is clear that the sabers are drawn. My father, a businessman, politician and former army captain, once told me a major international military conflict might be looming because "we have forgotten how much it hurts".

When I first visited Shanghai almost 20 years ago, two young university students approached me at an outdoor bar and asked if they could join me. At that time, as most people who spent time in China back then probably remember, it was common for students to initiate conversations with Westerners to practice their English and get an insight into life outside China. For me, these types of conversations have often afforded invaluable glimpses into people's lives and dreams. The two students were very friendly and we got along fine. Then, suddenly, the conversation took an unexpected turn.

"I'm happy China's getting richer," said the young man, who was studying Chinese history. "Because then we can build a strong army – and once and for all crush Japan."

"And after that the Americans," said the woman, who studied international politics, with a smile.

What worries me today is that comments along similar lines are becoming more and more common, not just from Chinese but from Americans too. A tremendous degree of military tension has been building over the last few years. China has militarized disputed groups of islands in the South China Sea and made repeated provocations against Taiwan. There's a border conflict with India, as well as warship standoffs with the US Navy in disputed waters. Chinese TV plays, on loop, war movies in which the PLA kills Japanese soldiers, while the news constantly portrays the growing might of the Chinese military.

The conflict between the US and China is not solely the making of Donald Trump and Xi Jinping. It's something that has been brewing for decades, a conflict that's now flaring up more forcefully and aggressively than many had anticipated. As shown earlier, surveys from both the Pew Research Center and Harvard CAPS-Harris indicate that an increasing number of people in the US view China as an enemy. If terror organizations such as Al-Qaeda kept people awake at night before, the rise of China is today considered the most serious danger to the American way of life. The director of the FBI, Christopher Wray, has said that acts of espionage and theft by China's government pose the "greatest long-term threat" to the future of the US.

Similarly, a study published in 2019 – based on five surveys of Chinese citizens, internet users and elites – found that Chinese attitudes toward foreign disputes have grown more hawkish than dovish. This is especially true of the younger generation. Other research, although disputed, suggests that rising nationalism is a cause of China's increasingly assertive foreign policy, including its approach to territorial disagreements. The dynamic is quite simple, according to Adam Ni, a China researcher at the Department of Security Studies and Criminology at Macquarie University in Sydney: China is becoming richer and more powerful, and as a result its citizens are more proud, and this is reflected in China's new-found confidence.

Not long ago, an acquaintance of mine from Mainland China who now lives in Hong Kong, confessed to me that he's not a massive supporter of the Chinese Communist Party, and that this was one of the reasons he wanted his son to grow up in the semi-autonomous city. He added, however, that when the West threatens "the Motherland", there's no doubt where his loyalty lies.

To look at the equation from a Chinese geopolitical perspective, the conflict is often explained with reference to the notion that the US, and to some extent Europe too, wishes to prevent China from regaining its historic position as Asia's leading nation. The conflict has therefore often been described using the theory of 'Thucydides' trap', a dangerous dynamic that occurs when a rising power threatens to displace a ruling power.

It was the rise of Athens and the fear that this instilled in Sparta that made war between the two inevitable, the ancient Greek historian Thucydides concluded. The past 500 years alone have seen 16 cases in which a rising power threatened to displace a ruling one. Twelve of these ended in war.

Already in 2013, Xi Jinping was declaring in a speech to Western businessmen: "We all need to work together to avoid the Thucydides trap – destructive tensions between an emerging power and established powers."

When Deng Xiaoping initiated China's fast march to the market in 1978, he announced that the Chinese would "bide our time and hide our capabilities," which Chinese military officers have often interpreted to mean getting strong before getting even. Now, with the arrival of China's new paramount leader, Xi, the era of "hide and bide" is over. And America is seen as an obstacle to China's rise.

China has the world's second-largest military budget – far behind that of the United States, according to the Stockholm International Peace Research Institute. Measured in purchasing power parity, however – that is, in terms of how many cannons and boots one can afford in local prices – China's military budget has already reached 87 percent that of the US, according to the conservative think tank The Heritage Foundation.

Now, to understand how China sees itself in the world, let's recall the words of Singapore's late leader, Lee Kuan Yew. Few people understood China better than LKY. He was a mentor to Chinese leaders from Deng Xiaoping onwards and a strategic counselor to many presidents and prime ministers, including every American head of state from Richard Nixon to Barack Obama.

"The size of China's displacement of the world balance is such that the world must find a new balance," he said. "It is not possible to pretend that this is just another big player. This is the biggest player in the history of the world."

On the question of whether China's leaders are serious about displacing the United States as the top power in Asia in the foreseeable future, Lee answered directly: "Of course. Why not … how could they not aspire to be number one in Asia and in time the world?"

And what of China accepting its place in an international order designed and led by America? Absolutely not: "China wants to be China and accepted as such – not as an honorary member of the West."

America, Lee added, would find this adjustment uncomfortable. Oh, indeed.

THE GREAT SELLOUT

"The US has lost the knowledge needed to manufacture the cutting-edge products it invented"

American politicians consistently blame China for stealing American technology and killing American jobs. But you might just as soon conclude that American companies gave it away.

The outsourcing wave that has, over the last decades, moved apparel production to China and call center operations to India, is at the heart of America's trade imbalances and the astounding technological advancement of Asia. A quick Google search reveals stacks of articles and blog posts with titles like: "Will Outsourcing Kill America?"

It's not rocket science. When a company outsources production to a faraway country it loses its connection to the manufacturing floor and its genius for doing and making. The knowledge is transferred to workers in the new country. Next follow research and development – which is where the true magic happens in any engineering company. And when the bulk of the company's

R&D has moved away, innovation follows. This is – partly – why China's factory workers and engineers are so goddamn good at what they do. As production sailed away from Europe and America, China and other emerging markets sucked up know-how. And that, together with China's unabashed can-do spirit and well-developed education system, laid the foundation for it becoming an innovation powerhouse.

In a prescient Harvard Business Review article, two Harvard professors, Gary Pisano and Willy Shih, assert: "The US will finally have to take the problem seriously. Rebuilding its wealth-generating machine – that is, restoring the ability of enterprises to develop and manufacture high-technology products in America – is the only way the country can hope to pay down its enormous deficits and maintain, let alone raise, its citizens' standard of living."

Their article, 'Restoring American Competitiveness', stressed that America's relentless outsourcing of manufacturing operations had not only hurt the United States' trade balance and job prospects for its citizens, but also hindered its ability to innovate. "In reality, the outsourcing has not stopped with low-value tasks like simple assembly or circuit-board stuffing," the authors said. "Sophisticated engineering and manufacturing capabilities that underpin innovation in a wide range of products have been rapidly leaving too.

"As a result, the US has lost or is in the process of losing the knowledge, skilled people, and supplier infrastructure needed to manufacture many of the cutting-edge products it invented."

The article was published in 2009.

Since then, China has only grown stronger. To this, add that it has routinely demanded tech transfers from foreign companies doing trade and production on Chinese soil. And Western firms have willingly opened their IP closets to their future competitors.

Outsourcing is a tricky balancing act, both for individual companies and governments. Of course, it helps Western companies to be more competitive in the global marketplace, and allows them to sell to foreign markets. It has helped companies to cut costs and nations to keep inflation in check. As old industries and less-skilled jobs have disappeared, some countries have been successful in lifting their citizens to higher-skilled jobs. Yet others have not, which in many cases has led to hardship in local communities and even resentment toward governments, globalization and big finance.

Or, as one MIT Technology Review article laid out the dynamic: If one fisherman doubles his effort, he can double his income, but if all of them double their effort, the fishery will be rapidly depleted. In the context of outsourcing manufacturing, when too many companies do it, the local industrial ecosystem suffers long-term consequences.

Sweden's foreign trade minister, Anna Hallberg, recently told me in an interview: "We're an entrepreneur-driven economy, and we are stepping up higher in the value chain with a more advanced working force. To start [the discussion with] where production should be made feels slightly obsolete and old-fashioned."

But I also remember the words of Mauro Gozzo, chief economist at the trade promotion organization Business Sweden. When I had the pleasure of working with him briefly, some 20 years ago, he told me that relocating production sometimes increases a company's competitiveness, but that it comes with a price, namely that you leave production and much of your decision-making to strangers on the other side of the globe. Strangers who "promise" not to copy or take advantage of your inventions.

If you don't mind, I'd like to recount something of a parable.

> One sunny afternoon some 4,600 years ago, the Chinese empress Leizu, wife of the Yellow Emperor, was strolling through the royal garden when a cocoon suddenly dropped down in her teacup. When she picked it up, she found that she could unwind soft threads around her finger. According to legend, this is how silk was discovered.
>
> The details of silk production were kept a closely-guarded secret within China for over 2,000 years, during which time it became the country's most

important and lucrative export commodity. In Rome, demand was so high that it almost broke the city's finances. Governments and tradesmen all over the world were desperate to discover the secret of how silk was made, but in China an imperial decree carried a death sentence for anyone caught exporting silkworms or their eggs.

Now, imagine that one of the Chinese emperor's advisers had approached him with an idea: Let's outsource the production of silk to Rome.

"But if we share our secret with the Romans, how can we be sure that they won't steal it?" the Emperor might have asked.

The advisor tells the Emperor not to worry. "I'll make them sign an intellectual property agreement. They will have to promise to follow our rules and not take unfair advantage of our trust. I'm sure we can trust them."

Would you have accepted the advisor's advice? The Emperor declines - and China's monopoly on silk is maintained for another millennia or two.

Eventually, the secret leaked. In the 15th century, the Italian city of Como became the epicenter of production of silk and high fashion.

But then, just a few decades ago, a consultant approached the main silk business owners of Como with a proposal: "Let's outsource our silk production to China. I'll make them sign an intellectual property agreement. They will have to promise to follow our rules."

And the Italian business owners went along with the idea. Today, China is once again the world's biggest producer of silk. Meanwhile, many of Como's silk factories and fashion houses stand empty.

From this perspective, then as today, China has been considerably better at protecting its industries. As one China watcher has put it: Protectionism may be rising around the world, but in China it never went away.

EMPTYING THE CAGE

*"The factories close, guest workers move, restaurants
and shops close"*

"Don't be fooled by the trade deal between America and China
– The planet's biggest break-up is under way." That was the
headline of a leader in The Economist's second edition of 2020.

Just days later the emergence of a novel coronavirus hit the
news, along with allegations that China had tried to cover it up
– and global diplomatic and trade relations were pushed into
the gutter for real.

But let's reverse the tape. A trend of companies leaving China
had been underway for years, long before the trade war and the
covid-19 crisis.

Some years ago, I wrote a story comparing two neighboring
Chinese cities: ultramodern Shenzhen, nicknamed 'Asia's Silicon
Valley', and Dongguan, a factory town known as 'China's Sin
City'. They are both situated in the Pearl River Delta, in the

southern province of Guangdong, bordering Hong Kong. If Shenzhen was the model citizen in the context of the central government's vision of a high-tech China, its nightmare scenario was a mere stone's throw away.

Dongguan had become known as one of the workshops of the world. Not long ago, it produced more than a third of the world's toys, along with mountains of shoes, furniture and other mass-market products. More than two thirds of the city's residents were guest workers from other provinces. Like many Chinese factory cities, it aimed to move up the value chain via robotics and automatization.

Instead, however, a ruthless wave of bankruptcies and factory shutdowns had swept through the city. With the number of minimum-wage earners having soared over the years, competition from other low-income countries such as Vietnam, Mexico and Bangladesh now presented a major challenge to their economic prospects. Also playing into the scenario were the central government's beefed-up environmental and sustainability requirements.

Guangdong's former provincial party secretary, Wang Yang – now a member of the Politburo Standing Committee – once used a metaphor to describe the change he desired: "Empty the cage and let the right birds in." But with the cage now empty, would new birds move in?

"No, it's not happening," said a local businessman whose company made furniture and who gave the pseudonym Han Yulai. After many successful years, the company had lost most of its export sales and let go many of its employees. "Just in the past few weeks I have heard so many factory owners planning to close down or move their production," Han told me. "They cannot afford to stay or are not willing to invest in more expensive production lines."

We drove around the city's factory areas for several hours. Everywhere we looked were empty or half-empty factories. Massive red banners, hung on the fronts of buildings, displayed phone numbers to call to rent or lease space.

According to Han, rents had dropped by half in only two years. In some parts of town, more than a third of all factories had shut their doors, he said. Factory owners were offering a finder's fee of a month's rent for information leading to new tenants. Many factories had been turned into other types of businesses - such as restaurants or department stores. We drove past a factory being used as a primary school in a contaminated industrial area.

"This is a catastrophe," said Han. "The government should stop factories from moving to cheaper countries."

And it wasn't just international companies who were pulling out. Chinese companies were also diversifying to other nations to cut costs and to accommodate demands from foreign buyers. Lost leasing revenues from factories and residential buildings were already causing burgeoning city debt. Migrant factory workers had also started leaving.

"This is a downward spiral," Han told me. "The factories close, guest workers move, restaurants and shops close. I am concerned for the future of my family."

China is also an increasingly difficult place for foreign manufacturers to do business, according to Boston Consulting Group. The country ranks lower than many of its Asian peers on international indices of commercial openness and bureaucratic efficiency, for example, and taxes on labor are the highest in the region. Back in 2000, Chinese manufacturing labor costs averaged only US$0.46 per hour – 53 times lower than the US$25 per hour average in the US. Since then, Chinese manufacturing labor costs have been rising by 15 percent per year on average – faster than gains in productivity, of 10 percent per year.

Dongguan's mayor, Yuan Baocheng, keeps up a constant effort in the media to project a positive image of the city. He says that massive investments are being made in robot automation and points to positive signs in the mobile-phone and high-tech manufacturing sectors. Today, with the help of stimulus from various levels of government, the city is attempting to reinvent itself as a smart manufacturing base focused on producing hi-tech robotics and automated equipment, all in the hope that the boom times will return.

However, many businessmen and observers feel the measures being implemented by the local authorities are "too little, too late" and that the situation has turned into a race for the bottom, as price competition intensifies and quality drops further.

After years of trade conflict and several months of the covid-19 crisis – both of which have laid siege to global demand – the situation has deteriorated not only in Dongguan but in many other Chinese factory cities too. Analysts have warned that China's supply chains and its status as the world's factory are about to fall off a cliff.

Jason Liang, sales manager for a Guangdong-based exporter of LED lighting products, told the South China Morning Post that his company had already moved some of its production overseas and predicted others would soon follow.

"We're so lucky we invested in a Thailand-based factory last year," he said. "I think this virus outbreak will spur more production capacity to be relocated abroad."

Several high-end apparel brands have also been turning their heels on China. Adidas has cut the share of its footwear made in China in half since 2010, and a similar story is playing out at Nike: A decade ago, China was Nike's main footwear producer; today, Vietnam holds that title. Adidas CEO Kasper Rorsted has commented: "I'm not going to rule out that this trend is going to continue."

Japan's largest fashion chain, Uniqlo, has increased its number of major suppliers in Vietnam by about 40 percent in the last year or so, as it looks for options beyond China. And Hong Kong's Esquel Group, the world's largest contract manufacturer of cotton shirts for global brands such as Nike, Zara, Ralph Lauren and Tommy Hilfiger, has set up manufacturing operations in Mauritius, Malaysia, Sri Lanka and Vietnam, diversifying away from its production base in Guangdong province.

In an interview some time ago, the company's CEO John Cheh told me that Esquel is "not leaving China". More recently, he has stated that the company's global supply chain has better enabled it to navigate the trade war. That was true, at least, until Esquel ended up on a US blacklist over its business in Xinjiang.

Yet another interesting example is Cao Dewang, the Chinese owner of the Fuyao Glass America factory that featured in the award-winning Netflix documentary 'American Factory'. He has warned that China's role in the global supply chain could be weakened and that global firms will cut their reliance on Chinese manufacturing after the coronavirus.

"After the epidemic, the global industrial chain will reduce its dependence on China," he told The Beijing News, a state-controlled newspaper.

"The global industrial chain cannot and should not decouple from China. However, we must self-reflect on the fact that, because of rising labor costs, trade frictions and other factors, the cost of China's manufacturing industry has been rising, making it lose its previous competitiveness. For example, some manufacturing enterprises have started moving out to lower-cost Southeast Asian nations.

"The decline of manufacturing competitiveness will lead to the decline of China's national competitiveness, and we need to be vigilant against such a trend."

What's quite clear is that the era for cheap and cheerful manufacturing in China is over. It's no longer cheap, and it's certainly not cheerful.

HIGH-TECH PULLOUT

"China's days as the world's factory are done"

Manufacturing of low-quality goods was the first to move out – and some analysts claim that most talk of decoupling, diversification and reshoring mainly refers to such industries. But that's wrong. It's happening in high-end manufacturing too.

Perhaps the most powerful case is that of Samsung Electronics, the world's biggest maker of mobile-phone and other everyday cutting-edge technology products. At the end of 2019, the South Korean giant closed its last mobile-phone factory in China – in Huizhou, another city in the Pearl River Delta. The move was portrayed in international business media as a massive symbolic blow to Chinese manufacturing.

"Samsung has achieved something that Tim Cook, chief of its arch-rival Apple, has suggested would be all but impossible: it has moved its smartphone manufacturing out of China," the Financial Times commented.

It didn't take long for the second domino to fall. In August 2020, the Korean tech giant confirmed that it is also closing down its last PC factory in China, in a move to cut costs and improve the efficiency of its supply chain amid rising geopolitical tensions. The move was seen by commentators as further evidence that China is quickly losing its advantage in assembly and manufacturing.

More local communities are taking a hit from the kind of manufacturing flight witnessed in Dongguan. According to media reports, Huizhou has turned into a ghost town since Samsung closed its three-decades old factory. At least 60 percent of local businesses have also closed up shop, according to the Institute of Contemporary Observation, which studies working conditions in hundreds of factories across China. The institute expects "at least 100 factories" and countless other small shops and restaurants to close down too.

Moving production out of China tends not to happen overnight. Samsung's pivot away from Chinese manufacturing chains, in order to "diversify the risks of its manufacturing bases", according to the company, has been a gradual process that began a decade ago. Step by step, it has lowered its dependency on China and moved capacity elsewhere. The move has also come amid rising political tensions between Beijing and Seoul, including Chinese boycotts of Koreans products and services.

The company's factories in Vietnam – a market Samsung first entered in 2008, lured by cheaper labor costs and huge tax breaks – today have a combined annual capacity of 150 million units, and make roughly 60 percent of Samsung's phones.

In July 2020, Samsung opened the largest mobile-phone factory in the world – yes, even bigger than China's notorious mega-factories – in Noida, India. The opening made a big splash and was attended by India's Prime Minister, Narendra Modi, and South Korea's President, Moon Jae-in. The new 35-acre plant will have an annual capacity of 120 million phones and also make other tech gadgets such as smartwatches.

For India, it was a significant landmark. In 2014, there were just two mobile-phone factories in the country; today there are hundreds. At the inauguration of the plant, Modi stressed that most of the phones produced there are for the local market, adding that Samsung's new mega-factory highlighted the successful blend of Korean technology and Indian manufacturing.

Its pullout on smartphone and PC manufacturing is not the end of Samsung in China. Indeed, the country's de facto leader, Lee Jae-yong, was one of the first foreign business leaders to visit China after the covid-19 pandemic took hold. The company is still investing in China, for example in a memory chip-making plant in the city of Xi'an. Chinese premier Li Keqiang recently made a surprise visit to the plant, saying he "welcomes increased investment in China by Samsung and other global high-tech companies."

Simultaneously, however, Samsung is increasing its chip-making capacity back home in South Korea, where it recently began work on a sixth domestic contract chip production line. This is part of a process of localizing the company's chip supply chain, a process that also includes strengthening ties with domestic parts manufacturers and local suppliers of related materials.

Samsung is also anticipated to be a beneficiary of ongoing tensions over 5G network equipment between China and the West. Why? Samsung builds all of its 5G equipment at home, making the firm unlikely to be hit by Western sanctions or Chinese retaliation, according to industry analysts.

Samsung's phones are far from being the only ones not made in China. Tech magazine ZDNet has listed ten popular handsets made elsewhere, including models from Taiwan's Asus, India's Moto, Japan's Sony and South Korea's LG.

Sure, it's unlikely that China will fully give up its place as the world's electronics workshop any time soon. But the outward-bound trend is accelerating. Many international tech giants are moving away from China, or leaning in that direction.

Alphabet's Google is moving some production of its Nest thermostats and server hardware such as motherboards out of

China to Taiwan, Malaysia and elsewhere in a bid to avoid US tariffs and an increasingly hostile government in Beijing. The firm has already shifted much of its production of US-bound motherboards to Taiwan, and has set up a new campus in Taipei.

"While Google's hardware production in China pales in comparison to the likes of Apple, its shift may herald a broader trend as tensions between Beijing and Washington escalate," Bloomberg wrote.

Quanta Computer, the world's largest notebook contract manufacturer and a major supplier of cloud hardware for companies such as Apple, Google, Amazon and Facebook, has also shifted production of servers out of China to Taiwan and to the US.

In 2019, the Japanese English-language business journal Nikkei Asian Review published a list of 50 companies that were pulling parts of their production out of China, partly in a rush to escape punitive tit-for-tat tariffs.

American personal computer makers HP and Dell are moving 30 percent of their notebook production to Southeast Asia, while the camera maker GoPro is pulling camera production for the US market out of China.

Japan's Nintendo is moving a portion of its video game console production to Vietnam. Other Japanese firms looking to move production from China include electronics maker Sharp, photocopier manufacturer Ricoh and Mitsubishi Electronics.

Not only are foreign companies rethinking their production locations, according to Nikkei, but a handful of Chinese companies are leaving China too. Chinese multinational electronics company TCL is moving its TV production to Vietnam, while Chinese tire maker Sailun Tire is transitioning its manufacturing to Thailand.

Now, let's come back to Apple and consider whether it is starting to reassess what constitutes "impossible".

China has been a critical factor in Apple's soaring market value, and its abundant network of suppliers and efficient, low-cost manufacturing base have helped cement Apple's profitability. But several experts and executives within Apple have for years warned about the company's dependency on China, and urged top leaders to rebalance its whole manufacturing apparatus. That dependency on China has become painfully clear during the pandemic.

"No executive will admit in a public forum: We should have thought about [the vulnerability to China]," Burak Kazaz, a Syracuse University supply chain professor and former researcher at IBM told the Wall Street Journal. "But from this point on, there are no excuses."

The company has started to experiment with production moves out of China, and many of its suppliers have stated that they are ready to make the shift.

Apple has already set up limited iPhone manufacturing in India, while production of AirPods has been shifted to Vietnam. It has tapped into factories in Brazil, and even made efforts to restart production of its Macintosh computers in the US. It has also reportedly asked major suppliers to assess the cost implications of moving up to 30 percent of their production capacity to Southeast Asia from China.

I often hear people saying that moving production of Apple products out of China could never happen because Apple is too deeply intertwined in Chinese supply chains. Some claim the price of an iPhone would double for the consumer if it was made elsewhere. That Apple would face hurdles in diversifying beyond China seems an article of faith.

But then again, look at Samsung Electronics. They have demonstrated it can be done. They have mega-factories elsewhere, and the company's mobile phones are in general cheaper (and better, I think) than iPhones.

Apple's top manufacturer, Taiwan's Foxconn Technology Group – which hires about 1 million unskilled and skilled employees in China – has said it has capacity to move Apple's production lines out of China if necessary.

"We are totally capable of dealing with Apple's needs to move production lines if they have any," Liu Young-way, chairman of Foxconn, told an investor briefing in Taipei in 2019.

He also recently said that he expects global technology supply chains to split into two camps: "It will be one for China and those associated with it, and another for the US and their friends."

Foxconn already has plants in Brazil, Mexico, Japan, Vietnam, Indonesia, the Czech Republic, the US and Australia, among other countries, and recent moves suggest it aims to sharpen its focus on expanding operations outside of China. Reuters has reported that Foxconn plans to invest up to US$1 billion to expand a factory in southern India.

"There's a strong request from Apple to its clients to move part of the iPhone production out of China," a source with direct knowledge of the matter told the news bureau.

The company's chairman, Liu, has even said that because of the trade war, China's "days as the world's factory are done".

Foxconn's production outside the country is now at 30 percent, a figure that's expected to rise as the company – officially called Hon Hai Precision Industry Co – gradually moves more manufacturing to Southeast Asia and other regions to avoid escalating tariffs on Chinese-made goods headed for the US market, Liu told Bloomberg.

Similar moves are happening with several more Apple suppliers: Wistron Corp, Pegatron, Inventec and others are all diversifying their manufacturing sites and setting up capacity in countries like Taiwan, India, Vietnam and Mexico. "We understand from a lot of messages from our customers that they believe this is something we have to do," Wistron's chairman, Simon Lin, said.

Despite the obvious signs that Apple and Foxconn are mapping out new manufacturing heartlands elsewhere, China's state-controlled broadcaster CCTV still says it's "a myth" that Apple production is leaving the country. For any seasoned China watcher, such statements are a signal of real fear among the country's leaders that it's actually happening.

YEAR IN A WORD: DECOUPLING

"Sorry, Davos Man. Your China-led globalization is going out of style like bell bottoms"

Some people still deny that decoupling is underway. They say it can't be done. They say we're too deeply rooted in China's manufacturing, too tangled up in its chains. State-controlled Chinese media almost daily deny that decoupling is happening, not in important industries anyway. And if it were, it would be disastrous for American and other companies. "US 'decoupling' attempt will be doomed to fail," China's English-language tabloid Global Times barked in June 2020. In a speech earlier in the year, Chen Deming, former Commerce Minister of China, said decoupling was unthinkable.

"To hell with decoupling!" Chen said.

And I guess it's natural that foreign company executives, analysts, fund managers and other China experts are reluctant to admit that what they've built up over the years in China may be losing its luster. They have skin in the game, so to speak. So do I, to be frank.

It's also true that some people are playing up the speed and importance of decoupling more than the reality on the ground justifies. Some do so for political gain.

The data is clear, however. Change is afoot. As mentioned earlier, even the chairman of Foxconn says China's days as the world's factory are done. It's not happening overnight, but it's happening. Meanwhile, China is stepping up its game to lure high-end companies to invest in the country and, more importantly, to become self-reliant in strategic industries.

Now, let's jump straight into the reservoir of data, surveys and academic insights.

• In terms of share of global manufacturing, the movement away from China is evident. A yearly study by the international manufacturing consulting firm Kearney shows that China, year by year, is losing its position as the world's biggest maker of goods. It's a fascinating read. The so-called Kearney China Diversification Index (CDI) tracks the shift in US manufacturing imports away from China and to other Asian countries. It concludes that while China remains the world's primary producer of manufactured goods, it has now lost share within the CDI for the sixth year in a row.

In short: China still leads the pack but it is losing share, and fast.

In 2013, the base year for the CDI, China produced 67 percent of all US-bound Asian-sourced manufactured goods. By the second quarter of 2019, its share had collapsed to 56 percent, a decrease of more than 1,000 basis points.

Of the US$31 billion in US imports that shifted away from China, almost half (46%) was absorbed by Vietnam, sometimes by Chinese suppliers who had left China, the report shows. Vietnam exported an additional US$14 billion worth of manufactured goods to the US in 2019, versus 2018, as a result of that shift.

"Sorry, Davos Man. Your China-led globalization is going out of style like bell bottoms," Forbes' senior contributor Kenneth Rapoza wrote in a comment on the Kearney report. It's a comment that perhaps summarizes this chapter – possibly even the whole book – better than anything.

Trade between the US and China has been dramatically disrupted by the trade war. China's imports from the US fell by a fifth in 2019 from a year earlier, while US exports to China fell too. For obvious reasons, trade kept plummeting as covid-19 broke out, limiting global demand.

• A study published in August 2020 by Baker McKenzie, a law firm, and Silk Road Associates, an economic consultancy, also shows how China's share of global exports is falling as international companies rethink their supply chains.

In 2019, Chinese exports of 1,200 products accounted for 22 percent of the world's exports, 3 percentage points down on the previous year, the report said. In consumer goods, the country's global market share fell by 4 percentage points to 42 percent. The difference was picked up across Southeast Asia, Latin America and Europe. There were also notable swings away from China in areas including computer hardware and audiovisual and comms tech exports.

• Arguably, decoupling from China is part of the de-globalization trend that has been unfolding for some time. International trade was stagnating before the pandemic, and global foreign direct investments (FDI) had fallen by 31 percent in 2019 from their peak in 2007, according to the bank BNP Paribas. The virus outbreak has sped up reshoring as a risk management measure, especially for the production of strategic goods.

The bank said: "The process of de-globalization forcing supply chain restructuring and decoupling from China may well continue, but it will unfold only slowly. It may lead to the emergence of two competing trading (and technology) blocs in the long term, with one led by China and the other led by the US. Such an outcome will reshape the global trade and technology landscape and have far-reaching investment implications".

• A report by Bank of America from February 2020 concluded that a range of reasons have led to an "exodus" from China's supply chains. Companies in two-thirds of global sectors in North America have either implemented or announced plans to pull at least a portion of their supply chains out of China. "Unsurprisingly, our survey validates the conjecture that a lot of companies are moving production facilities out of China," the bank said.

The report concluded that the trade war is only part of the story: Rising wages, stricter environmental norms, a complex regulatory framework, and the Chinese government's focus on creating a high-skill, service-oriented economy have combined to spur manufacturing exits, starting from a decade ago.

BoA also added the key point that Chinese companies in global sectors have also started to warm to the idea of establishing or expanding supply chains in the markets where their end consumers reside. Although Southeast Asia and India are preferred locations, some manufacturing is moving back to North America, the report said.

• A poll of 200 companies with global supply chains conducted by sourcing specialists Qima found that a staggering 95 percent of respondents in the United States planned to change suppliers away from China. The survey, published in June 2020, suggests a sharp uptick in demand among big American companies for goods not made in China.

Top destinations of choice were Vietnam, cited by half of all US respondents, and South Asia. The same survey found that fewer than half of European Union respondents had immediate plans to shift their sourcing, suggesting, Qima concluded, that the crux of the problem lies mainly in the US-China rivalry.

• The American Chamber of Commerce in Shanghai found in May 2020 that 40 percent of its members were considering relocating, or had already relocated, "some or all" manufacturing facilities outside of China. A clear majority said the increases in tariffs on both sides were having a negative impact on their businesses. Some, though not many, were even considering exiting the Chinese market altogether.

For companies that are moving manufacturing out of China, Southeast Asia, Mexico and India are the top destinations. Almost 6 percent of AmCham's members said they had relocated or were considering relocation of manufacturing to the US.

• European companies are also in relocation mode, although less vigorous about it than their American counterparts. They share worries about the business environment in China becoming increasingly hostile toward foreign companies. Joerg Wuttke, president of the European Union Chamber of Commerce in China, has said the coronavirus has made many businesses realize the need to diversify into other countries and avoid "putting all their eggs in one basket", and that company leaders have woken up to the fact that everyone needs a Plan B. Wuttke, who is also the chief representative in China of German petrochemicals giant BASF, told the South China Morning Post: "You must have a good eye on diversity. And the China story, the only story, possibly is over."

Meanwhile, Chinese foreign direct investment (FDI) in the European Union declined for a third straight year in 2019, according to a report by the Rhodium Group and the Mercator Institute for China Studies. That represents the lowest investment level since 2013 and a drop of 69 percent from the peak in 2016.

• According to a survey by the American Chamber of Commerce in Singapore, 28 percent of those polled said they are setting up, or already using, alternative supply chains to reduce their dependence on China.

• Small firms are also having a change of heart. A majority (56%) of North American small business owners surveyed by OFX, a global money transfer operator, said they are considering switching supply out of China, or have already done so.

"You have a couple of big names already moving to Mexico, all auto parts," Alfred Nader, president of OFX North American in San Francisco told Forbes. "Some of them are leaving China and going to Mexico because of the new NAFTA. Mexico has a nice supply chain in auto and they are decent sized players in textiles and in other industries that require light manufacturing. Most people don't really think of this, but Mexico is cheap and on a labor perspective it is as cheap or cheaper than China."

• In Hong Kong, nearly four in ten members of the American Chamber of Commerce are considering relocating due to the controversial national security law, a recent survey found. Thirty-nine percent said they are moving capital, assets or operations out of the city in yet another indication of rising corporate fears over the sweeping new legislation, which, diplomats say, has undermined the city's autonomy and independent judiciary. The New York Times has confirmed it's relocating staff from Hong Kong to Seoul, and I hear other international media companies are weighing similar plans.

"China was the biggest winner from globalization, which of course means it will be the greatest loser from de-globalization," Bloomberg has stated.

On the other side of the equation, other manufacturing countries are ramping up business.

Vietnam's share of world exports in consumer goods – from tech gadgets and textiles, to furniture and umbrellas – has increased over the last decade as companies have shifted production out of China. The country's share of textile exports rose from 5.9 percent in 2015 to 8.9 percent last year, while China's fell from 38.3 to 29.1 percent, according to a report by the market research firm Fitch Solutions. Some major tech giants, such as Apple, Google and Microsoft, have begun production in Vietnam, as mentioned earlier. In fact, Vietnam has enjoyed Asia's highest increase in global market share of manufacturing over a five-year period, according to a report by the Carnegie Endowment for International Peace. At the same time, inflows of foreign direct investment from China to Vietnam rose massively in 2019.

Other countries, like Bangladesh, Cambodia, Indonesia, and Malaysia, have also seen rising export shares in the period.

Meanwhile, according to Bloomberg, India's government has earmarked a land area twice the size of Luxembourg to lure businesses moving out of China. The country has even reached out to more than 1,000 American companies, hoping to lure them to relocate from China. There are also massive boycotts raging against China-made products in India, something we'll dive in to later in this book.

In the US, the White House has been "turbocharging" an initiative to remove global industrial supply chains from China and create a new alliance of "trusted partners" dubbed the 'Economic Prosperity Network', according to Reuters. Secretary of State Mike Pompeo has said the US government is working with Australia, New Zealand, India, Japan, South Korea and Vietnam to "move the global economy forward". Latin America may play a role, too. The urgency to depend less on China is not to be under-estimated.

Joe Biden has also stressed the need for better co-operation among allies. Creating a new transatlantic trade and technology framework would be top of his agenda, while a move to better align interests of like-minded nations would further strengthen the push against China. Europa, Japan, South Korea, Australia and other countries all share many concerns about the Chinese surveillance state and how its tech influence and propaganda is spreading globally. Donald Trump's biggest mistake, some experts have said, was to try to take on China alone.

For their part, Japan, India and Australia are seeking to build stronger supply chains to counter China's dominance as trade and geopolitical tensions escalate across the region. The Japan Times reports that the three nations are discussing building a "supply chain resilience initiative". Along with the US, the three are members of the Quadrilateral Security Dialogue, or Quad, an informal strategic forum.

A number of academic articles in Harvard Business Review have highlighted how American companies are navigating the trade war. "As de-globalization accelerates, two hostile economic blocs are emerging, one centered around China and the other around the United States," writes Michael A. Witt, researcher in international business at INSEAD in Singapore and at Harvard University's Reischauer Institute, in an article titled 'Prepare for the US and China to Decouple'. It's a short but punchy read in which Witt contends we're witnessing the opening skirmishes of a new Cold War.

He gives four brutally honest pieces of advice to American companies:

• Reduce your presence in Hong Kong. (The national security law will harm business.)

• Relocate supply chains to politically safer countries. (Relocating manufacturing to Vietnam might not suffice; better to move further away.)

• Re-evaluate relationships with Chinese companies and universities. (More Chinese organizations might get blacklisted.)

• Factor in the geopolitical investment risk. (Investments and economic development do not bring democratization.)

Again, some say decoupling can't be done. But as Bloomberg columnist Michael Schuman has pointed out, decoupling has actually happened before. In other words, this would not be the first time large-scale logistics networks, supply-chains and know-how have been built up in a new country.

"US companies have met this kind of challenge before – in China," Schuman wrote recently. "We've forgotten that the China we know today is very much the result of such hard work by international executives. Thirty years ago, reliable infrastructure, top-shelf talent, well-ordered supply chains and fat-wallet consumers didn't exist.

"It'll take work for corporate America to set up new supply chains and develop new consumers, but then again, the Chinese market took work, too."

If you are still in doubt as to whether the disintegration of US-China relations may be the most important economic event of our times, guess what The Financial Times picked for its 'Year in a word' in 2019. That's right: 'Decoupling'.

If the past 40 years were characterized by globalization, the next 40 may well be all about decoupling. The battle has only just begun.

THE SPLINTERNET

"The American and Chinese software and internet universes are heading at light-speed towards total separation"

China has for the last few decades been the epicenter of global hardware production, but it is also increasingly becoming a power player in software, competing with many of Silicon Valley's biggest names. The highest-valued tech startup is Chinese, and there are more unicorns – startups with a valuation of more than US$1 billion – in China than anywhere else. Chinese startup entrepreneurs are really good at what they do, and the user interfaces and features available on their mobile applications often feel fresher and more modern than those of Western apps. You know we're living in fascinating times when China accuses America of copying and stealing tech. Have you seen the deluge of TikTok clones coming out of the US lately?

The problem is that trust in these awesome Chinese software products is being compromised by the Communist regime and its obsession with collecting data on users – in China and perhaps abroad. Chinese companies couldn't legally refuse requests for data from Beijing, even if they wanted to.

When I met with Huawei's founder, Ren Zhengfei, last year he told me that Beijing had never requested the telecom company share data or open its backdoor. He repeatedly stressed that he would never break the trust of his clients. Other companies, such as Bytedance, the owner of TikTok, have also asked us to trust them not to transfer data back to Beijing. But how would one go about verifying their assurances? Huawei has been blacklisted in the US for more than a decade, although no hard evidence of espionage has been put forward. (More about Ren later.)

I for one have previously installed and used both WeChat and TikTok on my phone, but later deleted them. I have WeChat on a separate phone to keep in contact with friends in China. (Actually, keeping in touch with friends in the mainland is becoming increasingly difficult as communications apps are being blocked or privacy compromised.)

Much has already been written about China's dystopian system of mass surveillance. It's a system that should scare everyone. In Beijing, "every corner of the capital" is now covered by CCTV surveillance cameras, many powered with articular intelligence and facial recognition, according to the Beijing Public Security Bureau. The massive quantities of data generated from the myriad apps and digital services people use is what drives China's so-called Social Credit system, a controversial arrangement where citizens are rewarded or punished according to their scores. Millions of people have already been blocked from buying airplane tickets and joining dating sites. They are being named and shamed online. Some have even had their pets taken away from them.

"If you're born in a prison, and have been living in this prison all your life, do you know you're in a prison?," a woman I met in the city of Guangzhou asked me rhetorically a few years ago.

Other people in China say they like the surveillance and social credit system. It makes them feel safe, they say. As if they have a choice.

Surveillance – or simply spying – has become a booming business, with scores of tech startups moving in to meet market demand with the government's encouragement. Or, as Bloomberg put it in an article listing China's top companies connected to Beijing's mass surveillance: "In China, Big Brother is big business."

Dozens of China's most prominent companies – including AI-focused startups Megvii and SenseTime, video camera vendor Hikvision and gene sequencing firm BGI – have been blacklisted by the US government for helping local authorities surveil, repress, and detain mass numbers of Muslim Uighurs in the country's Xinjiang region.

For Western companies, it could be dangerous to collaborate with such blacklisted firms. Relationships with Chinese tech companies, no matter how brilliant they are at what they do, have the risk of becoming morally and politically toxic.

Let me give an example: A few years ago, Sweden's legendary camera maker Hasselblad – whose hardware was used by American astronauts when landing on the moon in 1969 – sold out to the Chinese drone maker, DJI. The deal was initially considered a good match and a way for Hasselblad to modernize itself. But then documents emerged showing that DJI had signed a strategic partnership agreement with the public security bureau of Xinjiang. Does this mean that Swedish camera equipment is being used in the surveillance and oppression of the Muslim population living there?

Now, as Chinese tech firms and Chinese mobile apps have gained an increasing foothold in overseas markets, governments and intelligence organizations in countries around the world are raising red flags over privacy, as well as ethical and national security concerns.

Would you like China's authorities to have access to your data?

Dozens of Chinese apps have already been blocked in India, and other countries seem to be following its example. Donald Trump has lashed out both at Tencent's app WeChat, and TikTok, claiming they pose a danger to security and privacy. Video games might be the next target, according to several analysts. Shenzhen-based Tencent is the world's biggest gaming company and has stakes in American companies such as Epic Games, Riot Games and Activision Blizzard, as well as in Snap, Reddit, Tesla, Spotify and many more. These might all find themselves caught up in the crossfire.

Meanwhile, several tech firms, including Google and Netflix, and media organisations such as the New York Times, Le Monde and the BBC, have already been blocked in China for many years. Censorship of outside information is rigorous. When trying to find the Swedish town Falun on Chinese search engines you'll get no results. Why? Because the meditation group Falun Gong is banned in China. It's like the government has a parental control setting on all of its citizens. Rather humiliating, when you think about it. Even the children's cartoon character Peppa Pig has been blocked.

China and America have never particularly connected online. American software firms made just 3 percent of their sales in China in 2019, according to The Economist, and China has long kept its internet users isolated from the world.

We're in a situation where Chinese apps and many Chinese tech firms seem to be stuck – or pushed back – behind the country's walled garden. Meanwhile, foreign media and online platforms are not welcomed in China. Some experts have called it a "virtual Berlin wall", or the "splinternet."

"The American and Chinese software and internet universes are heading at light-speed towards total separation," The Economist said recently in a leader article.

The software split is also felt among mobile phone makers. A new Chinese survey, involving more than 1.2 million respondents, showed that a staggering 95 percent of Chinese iPhone owners would switch from Apple to another smartphone brand rather than give up WeChat. As one user said: An iPhone without WeChat in China is just "expensive electronic trash". Likewise, millions of Britons with Huawei phones risk their devices becoming obsolete, as the Chinese maker can't use US software anymore.

"We are already in the age of the splinternet. I expect to see decoupling in telecom, internet and ICT services, and 5G systems," Robert Zoellick, former president of the World Bank and US trade representative, told a group of top US executives with business in China earlier this year, as reported by the FT.

"The best US response to China's innovation agenda is to strengthen our own capabilities and to draw the world's talent, ideas, entrepreneurs and venture capital to our shores," he added. "We will succeed by facing up to our own flaws, not by blaming others."

Blaming others, however, seems to be today's prevailing *modus operandi*.

Ian Bremmer, founder of analyst house Eurasia Group, predicted in a recent report that decoupling – which is already disrupting beneficial flows of technology, talent and investment between the US and China – will move beyond the handful of strategic technology sectors at the heart of the dispute, such as semiconductors, cloud computing, and 5G, into a broader array of economic activity.

"The decision by China and the United States to decouple in the technology sphere is the single most impactful development for globalization since the collapse of the Soviet Union", he concluded.

That's quite a statement.

"It will affect not just the entire $5 trillion global tech sector, but a host of other industries and institutions from media and entertainment to academic research, creating a hard-to-reverse business, economic, and cultural divide," he added.

"The big question: Where will the new virtual Berlin Wall go up? Which side will countries choose?"

In some areas, business interests are divided for logical reasons. You wouldn't, for example, share military secrets with or sell weapons to a rival. Now, development of artificial intelligence and other strategic technology might be considered within similar parameters.

Jacob Helberg, a senior advisor at the Stanford University Cyber Policy Center and former Google advisor, wrote in a recent opinion article that the coronavirus pandemic has "amplified and accelerated the thrum of a new cold war between an autocratic China and a democratic United States", and that tech is now being "weaponized", especially dual-use technologies like facial recognition and 5G networking.

As a result, he believes, American policymakers could increasingly view American companies that accommodate or assist the Communist party as unpatriotic and corrosive to US national security interests. Ultimately, they won't have much tolerance for US firms remaining nonaligned.

"Governments are beginning to eye global technology companies as proxies — and potential targets — of their respective national power; politicians are talking about artificial intelligence the way they once spoke of the atomic bomb," Helberg wrote.

"Sooner or later, US firms will find it untenable to remain neutral in this contest – let alone to accommodate autocrats in Beijing – while also retaining good relations with Washington."

Microsoft has proclaimed itself a "neutral digital Switzerland" and encouraged other companies to do the same. How much longer will it be possible to hold to that position?

ONE COMPANY, TWO SYSTEMS

"It is time for you to pick a side"

While some move out, others stay or move in. There are limits to the unwinding of relations. China pushes forward in technology, fast-moving consumer trends and the kind of smart city development that tycoons and business executives of Western nations will continue to want to share in. Many foreign investments in China today target the country's domestic market and its army of middle-class consumers.

Even here we find interesting trends reflective of the new world order of growing conflict and distrust, however. So how to navigate these new waters?

One way is through a corporate geographical split. As predictions of a world market divided into China and non-China start to become true, a trend is emerging of companies dividing themselves into China and non-China units – with one foot in the authoritarian territory and the other outside of it.

In the spring of 2019, I conducted an interview with the then-CEO of engineering giant ABB, Ulrich Spiesshofer, in Hong Kong. He was in town to participate in a Formula-e race (like Formula-1 but with battery cars.) As we walked through the sponsors' area, where ABB displayed its latest mini-robots and green energy tank stations, local staff flocked around Spiesshofer to take selfies as though he were a rock star. It was a big thing for his employees to have the head of the enterprise in town.

But it was a big deal for Spiesshofer, too. He told me he's not a massive fan of car racing, but saw the event as an opportunity to rub shoulders with the region's power players. If China's tech ambitions are a "direct threat to the United States", as the White house has said, they're a gold mine for ABB. The Swedish-Swiss company – which has been doing business in China since 1907 – makes roughly as much money in China as in the US today.

"If you look at the government's ambitions, and look at what the government wants to do with the country, it reads like a checklist for ABB," he told me. "Renewables integrations, smart cities with electric transport, industrial upgrade from automatization and robotisation: In all these areas, ABB is uniquely positioned to work with China."

He even explained that ABB and China are on a similar journey – a "parallel development" – in terms of their sources of competitiveness: from electrification and automatization, to digitalization of industries powered by artificial intelligence.

He said a recent meeting with Xi Jinping had been open and constructive and that the Chinese leader had explained the road forward for his country, as well as its global ambitions via the Belt and Road initiative, a massive and controversial infrastructure project in which ABB is involved in hundreds of projects. The firm will launch a new robotics plant in Shanghai in 2021, investing US$150 million, and has plugged into China's fast-growing market for electric vehicle charging stations.

Asked about the trade war, Spiesshofer said ABB would continue to expand in China despite the escalating conflict between Beijing and Washington.

A key to balancing the trade war is to have "fully integrated value-chains" in different markets. He explained that 90 percent of what ABB sells in China is being developed and manufactured in China. At the same time, most of what ABB sells in America is made in America.

He also told me that most top leaders at ABB China are local Chinese, not foreigners. Multinationals like ABB have over the last few years increasingly appointed Chinese executives, often Western-educated, to run their China operations.

"It's important to have your legs in different areas," Spiesshofer said. "We have a fully-integrated value-chain in America, and we have a fully integrated value chain in China. Our global dependence on complete product shipments from one side to the other has decreased, so we are basically naturally hedged."

In an interview with Nikkei Asian Review, ABB's chairman, Peter Voser, echoed that summary of how the company is navigating the trade conflict.

"ABB is a company which produces in China for China," he said. "And therefore global trade tariff discussions do not affect us in China. It may affect us when we go to the US, because in the US we produce 60-70 percent of what we sell there."

Ulrich Spiesshofer acknowledged to me that accusations of China stealing intellectual property are "legitimate", but added that the best way to avoid such theft is to "have constant innovation and stay in the forefront", and to develop unique tech for different markets. "In China we develop for China," he said.

This phenomenon has been nicknamed "one company, two systems" – a play on the "one country, two systems" policy under which Hong Kong is supposedly administered. It's a tricky balancing act.

In 2018, Harvard researcher Michael A. Witt conducted a survey of 109 board members of international companies. He laid out a Cold War scenario involving two exclusive economic spheres of influence, and asked the board members to come up with a strategic response. They were offered two major options: localize your business on both sides of the divide; or withdraw to one sphere.

To cope with the impact of the global conflict, and of punitive tariffs, companies are - according to surveys conducted by both the American and European Chambers of Commerce in China - increasingly adopting an "In China, for China" strategy to localize manufacturing and sourcing within China and serve the local market. It's a way for them to insulate themselves from the trade war while maintaining their ability to pursue domestic market opportunities and tap into China's innovation ecosystem.

The strategy of "one company, two systems" is an interesting concept – but controversial. As with the mounting signs that China's dual system, in relation to its administration of Hong Kong, is cracking, some critics say it's hard to decouple corporate values – especially in the midst of a geopolitical and ideological stand-off– without watering them down altogether.

In fact, the concept isn't new at all. Coca-Cola had a period of split personalities. In the 1930s, when Adolf Hitler rose to power in Germany and the Third Reich began, Coca-Cola – already by then an iconic symbol of America – found itself in a politically difficult situation. Like China today, Germany was a lucrative market. To fix the issue, the company took measures to re-establish Coca-Cola's reputation – not as an all-American icon, but as a brand fit for German consumers. The 1936 Summer Olympics in Berlin offered the perfect marketing opportunity.

"Just like with most brands active in Germany at this time, it appeared beside waving banners emblazoned with swastikas," Business Insider records, with reference to Mark Pendergrast's book 'For God, Country and Coca-Cola.'

Actually, the soft drink Fanta has its roots in Nazi Germany: Coca-Cola's German branch developed the soda during World War II due to embargoes that prevented the import of Coke syrup.

Today, several Western – and Chinese – companies face a similar dilemma in balancing business interests on one side and moral courage on the other.

One such company is TikTok, a video-sharing app whose infamy might be said to rival its fame. TikTok's owner, the Chinese company ByteDance, has been ranked as the world's highest-valued tech startup. TikTok is, however, blocked in China. There, ByteDance has a separate app, called Douyin. The two apps are clones: they have almost the same logo, interface and functions, and similar content.

The reason ByteDance released these two separate apps was so it could operate in China while expanding globally into foreign markets, too. It's perhaps the ultimate example of two-timing: a company stuck between two conflicting ideologies. One part of ByteDance is in compliance with international laws, the other is under the thumb of Beijing's censorship and propaganda apparatus.

Thousands of Chinese government agencies and Communist Party organizations are reportedly active on the Douyin platform.

The global popularity of TikTok has been a source of national pride. State-controlled Chinese media have said TikTok's success, especially its popularity among a younger generation of American users, stands as a representation of the true modern-day China and could help destroy the "evil China image".

To illustrate the company's schizophrenic condition, let's consider the decisions it has made in Hong Kong: The company closed down its operations in the city soon after the controversial national security law was implemented. It's a law that in many ways threatens freedom of speech, although the city's leaders say "one country, two systems" remains intact. ByteDance landed on the following conclusion: Hong Kong is not free enough for TikTok, and not authoritarian enough for Douyin.

At the time of writing, the White House has threatened to kick TikTok out of the US or have it taken over by an American owner, citing privacy and national security concerns. Facebook has criticized the app for alleged censorship.

The app has also come under fire from European regulators over suspicions that Beijing could force its owner to turn over data on its users. Sweden's public television and radio broadcasters SVT and SR have forbidden staff from using TikTok on their work mobile phones.

TikTok is already banned in India, the world's second-largest market for app downloads after China.

This is not the first time a Chinese tech company has presented two separate versions of the same app for China and non-China users. Shenzhen-based Tencent runs two different systems of its super-app: WeChat is the international version, Wexin the Chinese one. WeChat is targeted by American regulators.

Although I believe many companies will be tempted to create separate systems for China and overseas markets, in order to make profits in both, it's becoming increasingly difficult for business leaders to harmonize the rival interests involved.

Chinese e-commerce giant Alibaba is flirting with the idea of having one foot in each camp. I conducted an interview with the company's charismatic founder Jack Ma some years ago. As we stood in the garden of his private office in the Chinese city of Hangzhou, Ma beamed with optimism about how Alibaba was growing its international reach and how his firms could help companies and individuals across the world to boost sales and household income. But Alibaba has a tricky balancing act to pull off, as The Economist's columnist Schumpeter highlighted in November 2019. "It needs to keep the Chinese government on its side, but also appear less Chinese when winning over the outside world." The headline of the magazine's story? 'One company, two systems'.

One company that perhaps more than any other appears to have developed a dual-personality disorder is HSBC, a bank that's trying to pull off the seemingly impossible act of complying with contradictory regulatory commands from Beijing and Washington simultaneously.

The Hongkong and Shanghai Banking Corporation Limited opened for business under colonial rule in Hong Kong on 3 March, 1865 and in Shanghai one month later. It's today headquartered in London but makes most of its money in China and Asia. Its Hong Kong operations alone typically account for more than half of its profits.

As the trade war has ripped relations between China and the West apart, the bank today finds itself in a political and ideological crossfire between Beijing and Washington. Even its CEO, Noel Quinn, has acknowledged that HSBC has become a political target.

Chinese state media outlets have repeatedly attacked the bank. They have accused HSBC, for example, of colluding with the United States to build a legal case against the Chinese tech firm Huawei and its chief financial officer, something that has been a major flashpoint in US-China tensions. State media have even suggested that HSBC could be pushed "out of the market", or listed as an "unreliable" foreign company. Similarly, Western governments have lashed out at the bank. British lawmakers and some top investors criticized HSBC over its show of support for the national security law in Hong Kong. US secretary of state Mike Pompeo attacked what he called "corporate kowtows". Standard Chartered also got a whipping on similar grounds.

To manage the geopolitical headwinds HSBC is facing, as well as its problem of being trapped between the demands of the UK and US on one side and China on the other, one idea being floated by analysts is for the bank to split itself up and spin off its business across different geographies.

"With relations deteriorating and little prospect of an improvement, it may be time for the bank to consider separating its Asian business from the rest," Bloomberg columnist Nisha Gopalan wrote in an opinion piece titled 'HSBC's split personality is dragging it down'.

By creating two companies with separate management teams and perhaps listings, HSBC would stand a chance of satisfying government and legal expectations in different parts of the world, Gopalan argues.

Imagine, however, the mess from a branding point of view. Would HSBC have to change its slogan to "The world's local bank – except in China (and possibly other authoritarian countries)"?

The American videoconferencing application Zoom has also come under fire for having double standards. While the firm says its core value is to "deliver happiness", it's also complicit in Beijing's crackdown on free speech. It has developed technology "to remove or block at [a] participant level based on geography", and rolled out a model in which participants in China can be subject to censorship, but those outside of China can't.

Jacob Helberg, senior advisor at the Stanford University Cyber Policy Center, wrote in an opinion piece that firms like Zoom show "one company, two systems" doesn't work.

"The problem today is that tech companies that are based in the United States but also operate in China are struggling to comply with values that are fundamentally at odds," he said. "Unfortunately, some of the United States' major tech companies are still trying to sit on an increasingly uncomfortable fence."

He would know. Helberg is a former policy advisor at Google and witnessed up front how the American firm's Project Dragonfly – an effort to make a version of Google's search engine available behind China's so-called Great Firewall by conforming to the Communist party's censorship – failed and crashed.

"Tailoring one's principles to make them compatible with the CCP's dictates makes them systemically incompatible with American values," Helberg wrote.

A report from Citizen Lab found that the Silicon Valley-based Zoom was in fact partly developed by three companies in China.

The report called Zoom "a US company with a Chinese heart".

Zoom has admitted cutting off activists' accounts in obedience to China.

It has also shut down an international video conference commemorating the anniversary of the Tiananmen Square massacre. Prominent China watcher Elizabeth Economy was dropped from a Zoom seminar as she discussed China's oppression of its Uighur minority and other taboo topics. Organizations such as SpaceX, NASA, Apple, and Google have banned employees from using Zoom for work purposes due to security concerns. The US Department of Defense and the German government have similarly issued warnings and restrictions. The government in Taiwan has also banned Zoom from government business over security fears.

Zoom is, more than most other companies, stuck "between the principles of free speech and the power of China's huge censorship machine", as the New York Times has put it.

Would you call this a sustainable business model?

"Decoupling is increasingly accepted as the direction that trade policies are headed on both sides of the Pacific," Helberg opined. "With US-China relations currently more volatile than at any time since Tiananmen, it is an open question whether this decoupling will be slow and soft or hard and fast."American companies should prepare for what was once unthinkable: a sudden, hard decoupling in technology verticals deemed vital to national security."

Or, as Republican Senator Josh Hawley recently said: "It is time for you to pick a side."

FINANCIAL IRON CURTAIN

"There are plenty of markets all over the world open to cheaters, but America can't afford to be one of them"

"Let me tell you a joke: Yuan internationalization." Thus quipped a friend of mine who works as an analyst at a financial advisory firm in Hong Kong, in a recent text message.

He added a link to a Reuters story about Chinese banks panicking over US sanctions against Chinese and Hong Kong politicians and how Beijing fears being financially decoupled and stuck behind a "financial Iron Curtain".

"A sharp escalation in tensions with the United States has stoked fears in China of a deepening financial war that could result in it being shut out of the global dollar system – a devastating prospect once considered far-fetched but now not impossible," the story opened.

What has previously been referred to as the "nuclear option" in the trade conflict – cutting China off from the US-dollar payment system – is no longer unthinkable. The US also controls the main channel for international payments and clearing through Swift, the system used by banks to send money around the world.

Now, Chinese banks are desperately trying to maneuver after the US launched sanctions against some of the top leaders in Hong Kong and China – including Hong Kong's chief executive Carrie Lam Cheng Yuet-ngor – for their role in the alleged erosion of Hong Kong's autonomy.

Lam tried to laugh it off, saying she "[doesn't] particularly like going to the US". But the problem runs deeper than holiday preferences. Lam and her sanctioned colleagues face the risk of being cut off financially. Even China's largest state-run banks operating in Hong Kong have been taking tentative steps to comply with US sanctions imposed on officials in the city, according to Bloomberg. The banks are seeking to safeguard their access to crucial dollar funding and overseas networks. Major lenders with operations in the US - including Bank of China, China Construction Bank and China Merchants Bank - have turned cautious on opening new accounts for sanctioned officials, the news bureau said.

"Banks that don't comply with these sanctions risk losing access to the US financial system, which is of course an existential threat," Michael Hirson, from the consulting firm Eurasia Group, told CNBC.

It wouldn't be the first time the US sanctioned a Chinese

bank. Bank of Kunlun, for example, was punished in 2012 for financing Iranian oil shipments, and ultimately cut off from the dollar payment system.

Today, China strives to challenge the dollar's global dominance, with Beijing pushing for greater internationalization of its currency, the yuan. China has been buying crude oil from Iran using the yuan, and has been pushing Russia to use more yuan and fewer dollars. But its reservoir of clients does not run deep. The yuan's share of global foreign exchange reserves is only 2 percent.

"Swift and dollar dominance give the US a great deal of leverage over other countries," said the Foundation for Economic Education, a libertarian economic think tank, in a report. "A number of countries, including China, Russia, and Iran, have taken steps to limit their dependence on the dollar and have even been working to establish alternative payment systems."

Although China's financial system remains relatively closed, steps to liberalize it have been taken. For example, in May 2020 the American banks Goldman Sachs and Morgan Stanley, were allowed, for the first time, to take majority control of their securities joint ventures in China. International investors can also play the Chinese stock markets with ease. But the country still operates a system of strict capital controls - a system that can bring stability but also impede Beijing's goals of creating an international currency and expanding the nation's global influence, analysts have warned. Even Zhou Xiaochuan, former governor of the People's Bank of China, has said there are "advantages and disadvantages" to the government loosening its grip on the currency. Still, Beijing has to take actions to protect the country against financial decoupling.

"Yuan internationalization was a good-to-have. It's now becoming a must-have," Shuang Ding, head of Greater China economic research at Standard Chartered and a former economist at the People's Bank of China, told Reuters.

Beijing has no choice but to prepare for Washington's "nuclear option" of kicking China out of the dollar system, Shuang said. "Beijing cannot afford to be thrown into disarray when sanctions indeed befall China."

The ultimate sanction would involve US seizures of China's US financial assets; Beijing holds over $1 trillion yuan in US government debt. Not likely, but hey, we're in uncharted territory.

And Beijing's financial headaches don't stop at sanctions. Fears of a financial Iron Curtain have grown as Chinese firms are threatened with being kicked out of the American financial markets and with regulations that would limit US investments in Chinese companies. The White House has said companies from China and other countries that do not comply with US accounting standards will be delisted from the country's stock exchanges by the end of 2021.

Chinese firms are audited by Chinese auditors. US regulators and auditing watchdogs are therefore limited in their ability to verify the accuracy or quality of these audits. Even the head of the US securities regulator has warned investors against putting money into Chinese companies. There are more than 100 Chinese companies listed in New York, including tech titans Alibaba, JD.com and Baidu, and the energy firms PetroChina and China Petroleum & Chemical Corp. Now, Chinese companies face a choice: They could comply with the tighter regulations and remain listed in the US – or leave.

"The US regulatory system demands access to auditor documents, and China prohibits access to the documents," Brock Silvers, managing director at Kaiyuan Capital, a Shanghai-based private equity firm, told Nikkei Asian Review. "China may elect to have companies delist rather than allow them to violate Chinese regulation by submitting to US demands."

Republican senator John Kennedy put it in slightly less refined terms:

"There are plenty of markets all over the world open to cheaters, but America can't afford to be one of them".

CHOKEHOLD ON DRUGS

"Yes, China knowingly kept corona virus data secret"

The diplomatic turbulence that followed the outbreak of covid-19 threw global trust down the gutter, no question. Nation turned against nation, and actions taken by some leaders were nothing short of petty. But the squabble that broke out between Washington and Beijing trumps everything. The accusations, intimidations, lies and racial slurs flying out of the mouths of leaders in both camps have been appalling. It all quickly turned into a diplomatic disaster.

The White House stepped up its China critique on several fronts, possibly to cover up its own shortcomings. "This is worse than Pearl Harbor. This is worse than the World Trade Center. There's never been an attack like this," Donald Trump said of the pandemic. "It could have been stopped in China. It should have been stopped right at the source, and it wasn't."

Beijing, meanwhile, deployed an army of hard-line diplomats, so-called "Wolf Warriors", to spread hoax stories and intimidate national leaders and media.

I actually found myself in the crossfire. In an official statement, the Chinese Embassy in Stockholm "condemned" me for an opinion piece I'd written for Sweden's Dagens Industri newspaper. The piece was about how Beijing tried to distance itself from the virus outbreak and instead spread ridiculous conspiracy theories that the virus in fact came from other countries, including one suggesting that it was planted in Wuhan by the US military.

The Chinese Embassy called me "unscientific", which I found quite comical.

The Chinese propaganda machine is not to be taken lightly. When it comes to disinformation, Beijing has borrowed directly from the KGB cookbook. The purpose was not to convince people of one specific explanation for the virus, but rather to flood them with a plethora of contradictory hypotheses. Meanwhile, medical doctors and scientists in China have been silenced and punished. Beijing has kicked out international journalists to strengthen its own control of the narrative. A new report from the University of Toronto's Citizen Lab showed that the Chinese social app WeChat blocked more than 2,000 keywords related to covid-19. Early warnings about the virus were censored, as were domestic criticisms of China's handling of the outbreak, said the report.

The covid-19 crisis has highlighted how quickly global trust is destroyed. The first casualty in war is truth, as we all know. Donald Trump has also been far from trustworthy in his statements about the virus.

But the crisis has also highlighted – to the shock of some – how dependent most countries are on China for vital drugs and medical equipment necessary to fighting the pandemic and other illnesses.

Thousands of medicines found in homes and used in hospital intensive care units and operating rooms around the world are from China. Some estimates put America's dependence on China for some basic medicines, such as antibiotics, vitamin C, ibuprofen and hydrocortisone, at over 90 percent. Experts have warned that China could use this reliance as a deterrent against the US and other countries. In previous political disputes, Beijing has stopped sales of rare-earth metals, a key ingredient in everything from mobile phones to military missiles, and a sector in which it has developed a monopoly.

"The coronavirus outbreak has made clear we must combat America's supply chain vulnerabilities and dependence on China in critical sectors of our economy," said Senator Marco Rubio of Florida, an outspoken China hawk. "The coronavirus shows the importance of bringing all of that manufacturing back to America."

Among the American population – regardless of political affiliation – there is massive support for cutting dependency on China for medicines and biotech. A survey by McLaughlin & Associates, conducted in spring 2020, showed that a staggering 75 percent of Americans polled feel the US should end its dependence on China for medical imports, including things like N95 respirators. When asked whether they believe China kept information about covid-19 secret, 70 percent chose the option: "Yes, China knowingly kept corona virus data secret." The poll also showed huge support for mandating American firms involved in essential manufacturing and technology to depart China and "help rebuild the American economy".

Alarm bells had been ringing before the outbreak. In 2019, the US-China Economic Security Review Commission warned that the country's reliance on China as the world's largest producer and exporter of active pharmaceutical ingredients (API) put the health of Americans and the country's national security at risk. "Should Beijing opt to use US dependence on China as an economic weapon and cut supplies of critical drugs," the report noted, "it would have a serious effect on the health of US consumers."

Donald Trump's former economic adviser, Gary Cohn, argued months before the pandemic began that the US shouldn't anger the Chinese in a trade war because if "you're China and you really want to destroy us, just stop sending us antibiotics".

In the 2018 book 'China Rx: Exposing the Risks of America's Dependence on China for Medicine', the authors highlight two major problems with China's chokehold on drugs. First, it is inherently risky for the United States to become dependent on any one country as a source for vital medicines, especially given the uncertainties of geopolitics. Second, lapses in safety standards and quality control in Chinese manufacturing are also a risk. "If China shut the door on exports of core components to make our medicines, within months our pharmacy shelves would become bare and our health care system would cease to function", one of the authors, Rosemary Gibson, a senior adviser with the Hastings Center, told the New York Times.

European defense officials are also fretting about the national security implications of China's dominance in the active pharmaceutical ingredient sector, prompting some EU leaders to concede that the time has come to end dependence on China and increase domestic production. Jörg Wuttke, chairman of the European Union Chamber of Commerce in China, expresses the argument bluntly: "The globalization of putting everything where production is the most efficient – that is over."

Australia has also raised alarm. The country imports over 90 percent of its medicines, mostly from China, and is "at the end of a very long global supply chain, making the nation vulnerable to supply chain disruptions," a 2020 report said.

However, there is no easy fix to the problem. India is one of the world's biggest exporters of pharmaceutical products, but an estimated 70 percent of the active pharmaceutical ingredients (APIs) used by Indian drug manufacturers are sourced from China.

Building new factories elsewhere to ensure the supply of ingredients for essential medicines would be relatively straightforward. But it would "involve upending well-established political and economic theories, starting with the wisdom of allowing private companies to seek out the best-value goods, with little heed paid to their origin," The Economist said.

Such a shift will take time, but the wheels are in motion. Breaking China's near-monopoly on drugs will most likely be a top priority.

The US government recently awarded a 10-year contract to Phlow Corp, a Virginia company, to insure against drug shortages by producing ingredients and generics. In Europe, French drugmaker Sanofi SA is setting up an ingredients supplier with the aim of becoming the number two global producer, with annual sales of €1 billion by 2022. India is ramping up production of pharmaceutical ingredients to offer itself as an alternative supplier to China, and the government has announced a US$1.8-billion fund for setting up three drug manufacturing hubs. Indonesia has also announced plans to increase its production of pharmaceutical raw materials.

The issue regarding China's medical products runs deep, however. The direct connection between China's biotech firms and its government is a source of concern in itself. I'll give you a disturbing illustration of how.

One of the world's leading companies for covid-19 testing kits and related research, Beijing Genomics Institute (BGI), has sold millions of test kits to countries and regions across the world, including the US and Europe. But it's also integral to Beijing's mass surveillance of its people, according to several documents and statements I've been digging through. Two of BGI's subsidiaries have been blacklisted by the US Commerce Department for helping conduct "genetic analyses used to further the repression" of Uighurs and other Muslim minorities. Biotech and genetic engineering are part of Beijing's national strategy of military-civil fusion.

Intelligence agencies such as Israel's Mossad have warned against collaboration with companies like BGI over DNA privacy fears. But ultimately whether organizations in democratic countries should or should not collaborate with companies connected to human rights violations is an ethical question. Due diligence on Chinese firms today increasingly requires political checks and ethical caution.

"We should all be deeply concerned about BGI's work in Xinjiang," Emile Dirks, a PhD candidate in political science at the University of Toronto, told me. "Any country which partners with BGI runs the risk of appearing to condone the company's role in deepening state surveillance and repression in Xinjiang." During an online press briefing, I asked US Ambassador Philip Reeker, head of the Bureau of European and Eurasian Affairs, about the situation where European companies and organizations do business and collaborate with blacklisted Chinese companies. Reeker was clear: "We are watching closely."

For its part, state-controlled media in China continue to talk down both the threat and the risks of decoupling. In an interview with news bureau Xinhua, China's foreign minister Wang Yi summarized Beijing's view on Washington's actions against China with rather a notable metaphor, considering this chapter's topic of medicinal decoupling. "Acting like a sick person who forces others to take medicine for his own illness or even resorting to decoupling will not work," he said.

CHINA'S LONG MARCH
TO SELF-RELIANCE

"Let's fight tooth and nail to come out alive"

Although the government in Beijing and most of the country's business leaders favor globalization and open international markets (albeit without fully opening their own), they are also stepping up to the new challenge of being increasingly isolated and cut off from Western supply chains, especially in advanced technologies. One of the answers is to push harder for self-sufficiency. It is, in a way, the ultimate decoupling strategy.

Few people have seen this more clearly than Ren Zhengfei, the founder of Huawei. The Shenzhen-based telecom giant has become almost emblematic of the trade and tech war that's raging between the world's two biggest economies. More than perhaps any other firm, it epitomizes both the daunting rise of China's tech giants and a global trading system in which trust has collapsed.

Huawei has been a punching bag for American politicians for

more than a decade. It has repeatedly been accused – still without concrete evidence – of being an arm of the Chinese government and army, and hell-bent on spying on the world. Politicians in other countries have compared buying Huawei's equipment to giving China an "off switch" for a country's telecoms network.

As the trade war has escalated, so has the pressure on Huawei. The US has lashed out with a series of restrictions on the sale of chips and other technology to the company. In fact, the latest of these, at the time of writing, have been branded both a "deadly blow" and a "death sentence" to China's most important technology company if widely implemented.

On a sunny autumn afternoon in 2019, I sat down with Ren to talk about how he navigates the trade war, accusations of espionage, and the future of China Inc. We also spoke about the urgent need for China and firms like his to become tech self-reliant.

"First of all, we don't want to see de-globalization happen, we should firmly pursue globalization," he said, but added that Huawei is ready for a new reality.

"We can't change the world and we can't change our external environment, but we can change our own methods so that we can achieve success within the existing environment. A negative mentality could lead to failure."

Together with some Scandinavian colleagues, I met Ren at one of his company's massive new operational bases in south China – a lavish pastiche of a European chateau, decorated with oil paintings of the coronation of Napoleon, Roman pillars, statues of Egyptian hippos and even a full-scale Japanese village.

An old black-and-white photograph hanging on a wall serves as a reminder of the company's remarkable rise. It depicts the exterior of the company's first office, back in 1987: a shabby-looking apartment building in downtown Shenzhen. Under the photo a caption states: "Starting from nothing." Today, Huawei has four times more revenue than its closest competitor, Sweden's Ericsson, and higher revenue than China's best-known internet giants – Alibaba, Tencent and Baidu – combined.

Huawei is famed for its hardworking "wolf culture". It's an eat-or-be-eaten environment, according to several Huawei executives I've spoken with. Employees collapsing from being overworked have been hailed as role models.

However, after many years of constant success, many of Ren's employees, he explained, had become "complacent" and have "started slacking off". Now, the trade war has brought back their fighting spirit.

"With Trump brandishing his stick, our employees became nervous and aware that they must work hard to till the soil," he said. "Our employees were scared because he intimidated

Huawei. I also used to intimidate our employees, but the stick I used was not as large as Trump's. So his intimidation played a big role in driving our employees to work harder than ever before.

"I actually feel like I need to thank Trump."

Besides boosting morale, the trade war has also increased the urgency – not just for Huawei but for all of China Inc – of engineering self-reliance and developing indigenous technologies. The company has already lost access to Google's Android operating system and to the global supply chain provided by chipmakers such as Qualcomm, Xilinx and Broadcom. The situation is serious. Huawei's Rotating Chairman, Eric Xu, has said the company's topmost priority is survival.

Huawei is now searching for new supply chains and innovation partnerships to circumvent US sanctions. The government is racing to keep foreign enterprises in the country, rolling out the red carpet and dangling special benefits, while Huawei has stepped up its efforts to entice educated overseas Chinese emigrants to return to China, and to attract foreign talent. But more importantly, it's building its own replacement products, including an operating system and chips. Even if full decoupling with the United States remains unlikely, companies like Huawei are preparing for the worst.

Huawei has already started manufacturing and selling base stations that will power next-generation 5G mobile networks that it says do not contain US-sourced technology. The firm also says that its operating system, Harmony, is on par with Google's and Apple's ecosystems and that it is in a position to become one of the top ecosystem developers in the world. These are important steps for Huawei and other Chinese companies in developing an alternative software universe, and in chipping away at US leadership in mobile operating systems and enterprise software.

Leaning back in a Rococo armchair, Ren Zhenfei played down the suggestion that Huawei aims to be a rival to partners such as Google and established chipmakers. He said Huawei is "not seeking de-Americanization or trying to decouple from the US." He has said elsewhere, however, that the company can survive without the US. He told me that using homemade chips has been good for business, as it has lowered costs.

Asked if Huawei could one day become an exporter of chips, and compete with players like Intel, Samsung and TSMC, Ren kept his cards close to his chest: "We don't currently plan to do this."

Beijing, however, has grandiose plans for China to become a power player in semiconductors and all other sectors of strategic importance.

In 2015, China expressed its ambition to attain global leadership in high-tech manufacturing in advanced industries like semiconductors, artificial intelligence and information technology under its 'Made in China 2025' industrial modernization strategy.

"The world is undergoing profound changes unseen in a century, which are being accelerated by the covid-19 pandemic," Xi Jinping said at a symposium in Beijing on economic and social work in August 2020, calling for "breakthroughs in key and core technologies as soon as possible".

However, this ambition is nothing new. When the Trump administration banned the sale of microchips to telecom company ZTE in 2018 – taking the company to the brink of collapse – it was a wake-up call for China. Yan Ming, a director at the China Computer Federation, a research alliance, told the Financial Times that the sudden sanction "taught China a lesson". Now, the trade war has lent increased urgency to matters. In the race for 5G supremacy and technological self-sufficiency, funding is pouring in to the country's tech sector.

"Three years ago, there may have been more people thinking that we could rely on some US technologies rather than developing our own," Yan said. "Now if someone is still saying that, I suppose they have just been sleeping for the past three years."

Beijing is now accelerating its drive for "technological autonomy" to boost its control over its own supply chain in the face of political risks. The largest gap is in hardware, especially the design and manufacture of semiconductors and high-end chips. China accounts for 40 percent of the world's chip market by value, but its rate of self-sufficiency is only between 10 and 20 percent. Beijing aims to increase China's semiconductor self-sufficiency to 70 percent by 2025. Even if it fails to meet this target, it's unlikely to fall far short.

"When addressing foreigners, China's leaders talk piously of their commitment to free trade, market opening and globalization," The Economist has written. "Their domestic actions betray a different agenda: namely, to make Chinese companies dominant in high-value manufacturing sectors, and to hasten the day when they no longer depend on America for vital technologies..

"Long before Mr Trump was elected, China pursued such policies as 'indigenous innovation' and 'civil-military fusion'. Since Mr Trump's tariff war with China began in 2018, President Xi Jinping and his underlings have accelerated efforts to make China self-sufficient in high-value sectors, creating supply chains that are 'autonomous, controllable, safe and effective', in Mr Xi's words."

Last year, Beijing ordered all government offices and public institutions to remove foreign computer equipment and software within three years. That's an estimated total of 20-30 million computers. Good business for local players; for foreign companies an immediate blow. "We're being uninvited to bid. We're not being allowed to even participate any more," Cisco's chief executive Chuck Robbins is reported to have told analysts in August, referring to the company's business with Chinese state-owned enterprises.

China's 2017 Cyber Security Law also decrees that government agencies and critical infrastructure operators should use "secure and controllable" technology, yet another step away from global supply chains.

The Chinese government's latest move to reduce its reliance on overseas markets and technology is toward a so-called "dual circulation" model of growth. This model prioritizes "internal circulation" to boost domestic demand but may be supplemented by "external circulation". In other words, the home market is the top priority. The talk of dual circulation might sound diffuse, but I hear many analysts in Hong Kong referring to it as a serious way forward for China. One commentator said it smacks of the Mao Zedong-style self-reliance policy president Xi mentioned shortly after the US-China trade war erupted.

The Center for Strategic and International Studies (CSIS), a think tank based in Washington, has written that any new dual circulation strategy should be seen as part of "China's plan to push forward decoupling on its own terms".

"This further demonstrates that Chinese leaders are clear-eyed that bifurcation is not a question of if, but of when and how fast," it said. "The [strategy] was born out of a reaction to this diagnosis, and it is meant to posit a proactive strategy for China to shape the parameters of the divorce, not to shy away from it."

Analyst house Eurasia Group recently wrote in a report that Xi has realized that "decoupling is inevitable" and has called for a new Long March to break China's technological dependence on the US.

"Beijing's focus on building 'resilient supply chains' will raise the stakes of the US-China technology competition. That's bad news for US tech companies with big China footprints," wrote the group's founder and CEO Ian Bremmer and chairman Cliff Kupchan.

At the same time, China will expand efforts to reshape international technology, trade, and financial architecture to better promote its interests in an increasingly bifurcated world. "Trends of broader decoupling between the world's two largest economies will become more, not less, deeply entrenched as a result of the coronavirus, while other countries will experience greater challenges in balancing relations with both sides," the Eurasia group said.

By way of illustration, China's response to the conflict has involved a dramatic increase in support for indigenous innovation through initiatives such as its new US$29-billion national semiconductor fund and effort to foster a new Silicon Valley in the sprawling 100-million-population Greater Bay Area in southern China.

Regarding the hostility toward Huawei, some analysts believe that Beijing has little to gain from further retaliations against the US. Better to focus inward.

Dan Wang, a researcher at Gavekal Research in Hong Kong, wrote in a note that:

"China will refrain from major short-run retaliation, and focus instead on the long-run aim of building up its own semiconductor industry, to free itself from dependence on US technology."

China is also seeking alternatives and more self-reliance in other sectors. To reduce its dependency on the dollar-denominated financial system, for example, China has shown significant interest in developing its own blockchain technology and international payment systems.

Incidentally, China Inc is doing a pretty good job of catching up with – and in some sectors overtaking – the West when it comes to homemade tech. (This is something you can read more about in my last book 'Shenzhen Superstars – How China's smartest city is challenging Silicon Valley'.)

Already in 2018, a survey by the EU Chamber of Commerce in China found a majority of European companies believing – for the first time ever – that Chinese firms were either just as, or more, innovative than European enterprises. Who would have thought that a decade before?

If I were to point to one single factor that makes me think China actually has a fair chance of coming out on top in the tech race, it's the mentality of its people.

China's fighting spirit is awe-inspiring. I've witnessed the dedication and energy of her people several times at co-working spaces in Shenzhen and elsewhere. I even have a friend from China who lived in Australia but returned home because she found Westerners too "complacent".

Now, in times of crisis, this fighting spirit and determination to turn a challenge into an opportunity are perhaps greater than ever.

During the company's early days in the 1980s, Ren Zhengfei and his colleagues at Huawei knew that they had to work harder than ever before if they wanted to succeed, and they knew that they faced plenty of hindrances and hurdles ahead.

The company's slogan was: "Let us drink to celebrate success, but if we fail, let's fight tooth and nail to come out alive."

The time to fight tooth and nail has arrived.

LESSONS ON RESISTANCE

"Taiwan shows how to snip Chinese economic ties"

Most of the international attention in connection with the trade separation has been on the White House and its ambitions to bring back jobs and innovation and lower America's dependency on China.

Other countries have been cutting dependency on China for years, however; especially China's closest neighbors in East Asia. While Western nations have abruptly woken up to the fact that Beijing runs its own agenda and has no intention of being an obedient pawn in the US-led political and economic order, that's always been clear to most people in China's geographical sphere of influence. Some countries have already moved a long way in reshuffling their trade relations.

Japan is providing US$2.2 billion in stimulus funds to help Japanese companies move their manufacturing plants out of China, and the campaign almost immediately bore fruit early in 2020, with numerous companies getting onboard. Although the fund is relatively small, the signal and incentive are loud and clear.

Before resigning in August 2020, former Prime Minister Shinzo Abe made it clear that Japan needs manufacturing of high-added-value products to be shifted back to Japan, and production of other goods to be diversified across Southeast Asia to cut reliance on China. Roughly half of the first batch of companies to accept his government's offer moved manufacturing back to Japan; the rest relocated production to Vietnam, Myanmar, Thailand and other Southeast Asian nations.

"It is becoming clearer that too much concentration and dependence on one country is not desirable," Akio Takahara, of the University of Tokyo's Graduate School of Public Policy, told The Straits Times. "Such a principle of diversification will be implemented not only by Japanese companies, but by all, including Chinese ones."

South Korea is also pushing companies to reshore and relocate. As mentioned earlier in this book, Samsung Electronics is the lodestar here after it closed down its last mobile phone and computer factories in China.

At a high-level investment conference in Seoul in 2019, the main message was clear: We need to bring business back. Over several days, I spoke with and listened to numerous ministers and government officials throwing out incentives and special treatments for firms that choose to invest in Korea – Korean firms opting to reshore included, naturally. Tax cuts, cheap land, cash encouragements – you name it. According to Korean media, Korea Development Bank, Industrial Bank of Korea and the Export-Import Bank of Korea will launch a US$3.7 billion lending program for reshoring non-large enterprises.

Most other countries in the region have similar schemes to attract investments. Indeed, the best lessons are to be learned from Taiwan.

The self-ruled island – a major producer of technology products for the global market – has a strained relationship with Being. China and Taiwan – officially the People's Republic of China and the Republic of China, respectively – separated in 1949 following a civil war. China's ruling Communist Party has never governed Taiwan but claims the island as its territory. Taiwan sees itself as a sovereign nation, with its own passport, currency, legal system, army, democratically elected government and political and cultural identity.

A few years ago I interviewed Taiwan's then president Ma Ying-jeou in the capital, Taipei. Lounging in a dark-blue armchair under an oil painting of Sun Yat-sen – modern China's founding father – he delivered a clear message: economic relations with China should be developed but not at the cost of sovereignty.

"There has never been a country declaring independence twice," he said. "We declared independence in 1912, more than 100 years ago [when a 'Republic of China' was first declared on mainland

China]. There is absolutely no need to declare independence again. We now select our own president and our own legislature, and we are in charge of our own affairs."

At the time of our chat, the so-called 'umbrella movement' was raging in Hong Kong, and Ma gave his support to the push for democracy in the territory. He also urged Xi Jinping to introduce democracy for all of his 1.4 billion people.

Ma's critics felt, however, that the relationship with Beijing had become too cozy. After the so-called 'sunflower movement', where hundreds of students occupied Taiwan's parliament, new trade agreements with Beijing were subsequently dropped.

Since then, the relationship with Beijing has deteriorated considerably. Under the helm of current president Tsai Ing-wen, leader of the Beijing-skeptic Democratic Progressive Party, diplomatic interactions between the two capitals have ground to a halt. Xi has relentlessly increased military pressure on Taiwan, while the crackdowns on political freedoms in Hong Kong have sent chilling signals to her people. I was in Taipei for Tsai Ing-wen's inauguration, in 2016, and again in 2020 when she was reelected.

Around me, as I stood outside the DPP's headquarter and Tsai's victory numbers rolled in on a big screen overhead, thousands of people of all ages cheered and waved flags. Next to me an elderly man carrying his granddaughter on his shoulders told me, tears in his eyes, that he'd wanted her to experience what it feels like to celebrate democracy. In the crowd, I also saw several flags promoting democracy for Hong Kong.

"Taiwan is showing the world how much we cherish our free, democratic way of life, and how much we cherish our nation," Tsai said from the stage.

In the face of China's increased intimidations, Taiwan has "no choice but to continue strengthening our democratic defense mechanisms, and establish national defense capabilities", she said.

New trading and manufacturing strategies have also been central to Taiwan's resistance. China remains the top destination for its exports and outbound investment – but also its main strategic opponent. From the first wave of opening-up policies in China in the 1980s, almost 100,000 Taiwanese firms set up production in China. But over the last few years, thousands of Taiwanese firms have reportedly left China because of increasing labor costs, and Taiwan's government has increased a push for companies to continue the exodus.

Back in 2016, the government launched an ambitious plan called the New Southbound Policy (NSP), an effort to diversify Taiwan's economy and reduce reliance on China. In doing so, it was well ahead of the global curve.

The push has seen gains in trade, investment, and tourism between Taiwan and 18 countries in Southeast Asia and

South Asia, as well as Australia and New Zealand. Outbound investment by Taiwanese firms in these countries grew by 16 percent year on year in 2019. Meanwhile, Taiwan's outbound investment in China plummeted by 51 percent, marking a fourth consecutive annual decline in the measure, according to a story in Foreign Policy magazine headlined 'Taiwan shows how to carefully snip Chinese economic ties.'

Now, the government has sped this process up with a three-year reshoring initiative to help companies move their manufacturing back home from China. The plan – which especially targets innovative industrial sectors such as tech, smart machinery, biomedicine, and green energy – offers incentives covering land, labor, and energy, as well as tax breaks and bank loan subsidies.

The plan is working.

• Within roughly 18 months of its launch in early 2019, the reshoring initiative had seen Taiwanese companies pledge 1 trillion New Taiwan dollars (US$33 billion) to reinvesting in Taiwan, according to the FP story.

• This domestic investment by returning firms contributed to Taiwan's GDP increasing by 2.73 percent in 2019.

• The reshoring initiative is expected to create tens of thousands of new skilled jobs.

As mentioned earlier, the Taiwanese electronics contract manufacturer Foxconn has gradually expanded outside of China's borders and now says that nearly a third of its production capacity is outside of China, a figure that will likely keep growing due to the inevitable decoupling of Chinese and American supply chains.

"The global trend toward a G2 [group of two: America and China] is inevitable. How to serve the two big markets is something that we've always been planning for," Foxconn Chairman Young Liu told an investors conference in Taipei in August 2020.

"The forming of two sets of supply chains in the world is an inevitable trend in the coming future," he said. While India and Southeast Asian countries will become regional manufacturing hubs, he continued, "there will be no country to fully replace China as the global manufacturing powerhouse."

Foxconn's founder, Terry Gou, has even advised Apple to relocate investments from China to Taiwan.

Moving a fully integrated supply chain from one country to another is not done overnight, and Southeast Asian countries have a lot of catching up to do in terms of building manufacturing and logistics clusters as powerful as those in the Pearl River Delta or around Shanghai and Beijing. Firms from Taiwan and elsewhere are looking for consensus. But, as mentioned earlier, building a manufacturing heartland from nothing has been done before – and can be done again.

Either way, change is underway. Lessons learned from Taiwan can guide countries such as the US, Australia or the EU member nations in how to reduce dependence on China. Taiwan's government and people truly understand the urgent need to diversify away from China and have the will to do so – backed up by government-sponsored programs, as well as collaboration from the business community.

Taiwan's efforts have not gone unnoticed. Taiwan has significantly strengthened alliances with the United States, its most significant partner, and other "like-minded democracies", as Tsai has put it. The White House has reciprocated by showing increased support for Taiwan.

An overwhelming majority of people in Taiwan welcome closer Taiwan-US relations, especially economically. Nearly seven in ten interviewed in a 2020 Pew Research Survey said they held favorable views of the US, a considerably higher percentage than those who reported positive views toward China. Fully 85 percent of all those polled favored more US-Taiwan economic ties.

In terms of identity, the split with the mainland is becoming increasingly pronounced. Seventy years after the end of the Chinese Civil War, about two-thirds of adults in Taiwan identify as just Taiwanese, while a mere 4 percent see themselves as only Chinese, the Pew survey showed.

Many international companies have long been reluctant to do business with Taiwan in strategic or sensitive sectors, fearing repercussions from its mighty neighbor. That may be changing, however. In July 2020, Beijing threatened to put sanctions on US weapon maker Lockheed Martin in retaliation for Washington's decision to approve a deal to sell missile parts to Taiwan. But Rupert Hammond Chambers, president of the US-Taiwan Business Council, a lobby group, told the Financial Times that Chinese threats had not actually had any impact on American companies involved in arms sales to Taiwan. "They bark worse than they bite," he said.

Now, Tsai has said that starting talks on a bilateral free-trade agreement is among her priorities in strengthening relations with the US, Taiwan's key arms supplier. And the Americans seem ready to get such talks underway too. During a visit to Taiwan in August 2020, US health secretary Alex Azar – the most senior US cabinet official to visit Taiwan since Washington switched diplomatic relations from Taipei to Beijing in 1979 – stated that his journey recognized "Taiwan for its vibrant, open, democratic and transparent society… that contrasts with the conduct of the Chinese Communist party."

Beijing saw the visit, as so much else these days, as a provocation.

BOYCOTT AS
POLITICAL WEAPON

"Revolution Is No Crime! To Rebel Is Justified!"

An article headlined 'China's use of boycott as a political weapon' explains how Beijing deploys "pressure of economic resistance" and has been boycotting foreign powers for years in defense of its sovereignty.

"The story of the use of the boycott by the Chinese people is one of the most revealing chapters in modern economic history," reporter Dorothy J. Orchard wrote.

The article was published in 1930.

China indeed has a long history of using economic boycotts as a political deterrent. In 1905, it staged a large-scale boycott of American goods in reaction to a string of anti-Chinese incidents in the United States. "After the ball has started rolling downhill it will be difficult to tell when it will stop," wrote shipping magnate R.P. Schwerin to President Theodor Roosevelt about the decision by Chinese merchants to boycott American goods. A few weeks later, a missionary stationed in Shanghai warned that the boycott might "drive out every American and subsequently every foreigner". To a jubilant Chinese lawyer in Shanghai, the boycott was the "beginning of a new era".

The economic weapon of boycotting companies and countries is still commonly employed by China.

When the Nobel Prize was awarded to Chinese human rights activist Liu Xiaobo in 2010 – at a ceremony in Oslo where the award itself was famously placed on an empty chair, as Liu was in prison in China – the government in Beijing replied with an import ban on Norwegian salmon.

A few years later, the target was South Korea, in protest against the THAAD missile defense system. Chinese tourists shunned Korea, sales of Hyundai and Kia cars plummeted, and employees of the retail group Lotte were harassed in China.

Philippine banana farmers, Australian wine makers and Taiwanese tourism workers have all been on the wrong end of hostile campaigns.

The government in Beijing cancelled several meetings with British ministers after then-Prime Minister David Cameron's meeting with the Dalai Lama in 2012. French supermarket chain Carrefour was a target in 2008 after Free Tibet protests in Paris.

And last year Beijing aimed its ire at the National Basketball Association after Houston Rockets' general manager, Daryl Morey, tweeted support for pro-democracy protesters in Hong Kong.

Perhaps no one explained the situation better than Australia's former Prime Minister Tony Abbott, when he admitted that Australia's policies towards China are driven by two emotions: "fear and greed".

Foreign diplomats and executives dread the accusation of having "hurt the feelings of the Chinese people", the Communist rhetoric often used to trigger an embargo. "Their fears are heightened by China's growing economic might, the strident nationalist tone adopted by Xi Jinping and the fact that consumers are easily marshaled on social media sites such as Weibo and WeChat," the Financial Times wrote in an in-depth story about China's "boycott diplomacy".

The boycotts – or threats thereof – have often been successful. It's incredibly embarrassing to see how Western brands and politicians over and over again kowtow to China for the most minor perceived wrongdoings. The term "kowtow" dates back to the Qin dynasty, when subjects prostrated themselves in front of the emperor as an act of respect, kneeling and bowing so low as to have their heads touching the ground. It might be translated as "submission". Companies including the carmaker Mercedes-Benz, hotel chain Marriott, aviation company Delta Air Lines, clothing giant Zara and dozens of other international businesses have all bowed and scraped after being called out for having hurt the feelings of the Chinese people. Oh, the humiliation.

As the New York Times columnist Farhad Manjoo has put it: "If the first and most important cost of doing business in China is the surgical extraction of a CEO's spine, many businesses are only too happy to provide the stretcher and the scalpel."

Now, the economic shotgun known as the boycott is being fetched from the wall once more. This time the target is American companies, in retaliation for sanctions and other trade actions from the White House against Chinese companies.

Boycotts in China against Apple, for example, escalated last year as people felt they should show support for homegrown mobile phone brands. "There is a calling from my heart that I need to show support for Chinese brands, especially in the trade war climate," one netizen said. There are also loud calls among Chinese consumers to boycott Tesla. The Beijing government could decide to target both Apple and Tesla with trade war retaliations. In short, one analyst concludes, China could wreak havoc on these companies if it made the effort.

Data from FT Confidential Research, an independent research service from the Financial Times, showed in 2018 that respondents in China who favored certain US brands were quite willing to participate in boycotts. For example, a clear majority of consumers who picked Nike as their favorite sportswear brand said they would be willing to join a boycott. Starbucks drinkers and Walmart shoppers also said they would be happy to participate.

"Our data suggest a consumer boycott is a credible threat for some brands, should the central government decide to up the ante in its standoff with the White House," the report concluded.

International brands are now faced with a clear decision on how to manage a potential large-scale boycott and humiliation campaign from China: Continue the kowtowing, or show some courage.

It's becoming clear that a global pushback against China has gained momentum.

Many company executives and government officials have learned the hard way that they might have to cut reliance on the Chinese market to avoid boycotts, attacks and public humiliation. Japan, the most frequent target of Beijing's embargoes and boycotts, is one of the countries furthest along in adapting to offset potential damage.

"After the 2012 protests [connected to territorial disputes], many Japanese companies realized that our position in China would remain precarious, which has accelerated our move into other, friendlier markets like Southeast Asia," an executive from a Japanese manufacturer in Indonesia told the Financial Times.

Taiwan, South Korea and other neighboring countries have also come a long way in addressing dependency on China by pivoting key business interests to other fast-growing countries in South and Southeast Asia, or to Australia and New Zealand.

In the US, John Oliver, the host of a popular late-night talk show that takes a satirical look at politics and current events, used his influence to urge governments and companies to stand up for human rights in China and not bow to China's threats of economic retribution and consumer boycotts.

"Governments around the world should be speaking out against the treatment of the Uighurs without bending to China's economic influence", he said in an episode that focused on the mass detention of Muslims in Xinjiang province.

"Big multinational companies like Nike and Volkswagen should be working to clean up their supply chains and actively using their financial leverage to pressure the Chinese government to end these abuses."

Meanwhile, the Swedish singer Zara Larsson recently made global headlines when she ended her collaboration with Huawei to promote its smartphones, saying "China is not a nice state". In return, she was boycotted by Chinese fans – or at least that's what state-controlled media said.

Florida congressman Ted Yoho recently called on US citizens

to boycott Chinese products in support of human rights, citing Beijing's oppression of Hong Kong, Xinjiang, Tibet and Taiwan.

But the biggest pushback comes not from governments or celebrities but from ordinary citizens. A growing trend of boycotting products 'Made in China' is spreading across the world – from Mumbai to Miami to Manchester. On the back of general anti-China sentiment in the US and elsewhere, as described earlier in this book, there now comes a wave of sentiment against Chinese products.

A report from May 2020 found that 40 percent of polled Americans said they'd refuse to buy any Made-in-China products. The same survey, by Washington-based FTI Consulting, a business advisory firm, also found that 78 percent would be willing to pay more for products if the company that made them moved manufacturing out of China.

A clear majority said they favored raising import restrictions more than pursuing free-trade deals as a way to boost the US economy, while almost all respondents said the US is too dependent on foreign supply chains. This signals a major shift in attitudes as most Americans have traditionally embraced free trade and international commerce.

The findings were echoed by a Deutsche Bank survey that found 41 percent of Americans don't want to buy products made in China. Similarly, 35 percent of Chinese citizens won't buy products from America either.

I reached out to Laura Silver, senior researcher at the Pew Research Center, which conducts surveys on attitudes, to see if she sees any willingness among Americans to boycott Chinese products. She said that question hadn't been asked directly in surveys. But, she added, it wouldn't seem implausible: "We did find that a majority of Americans think that China is a competitor," she said. And, when it comes to the bilateral US-China economic relationship, Americans, by a margin of more than two-to-one, say economic ties with China are bad rather than good. Moreover, a quarter say such ties are *very bad*.

Similar sentiment can be seen in Europe. A survey from April 2020 by EUToday, a London-based, politically neutral media platform, found that 62 percent of polled Europeans would support a boycott of Chinese products in light of China's failure to alert the world to the true scale of the coronavirus outbreak. In the UK, an online call for a boycott had received more than 78,000 signatures at the time of writing. Several European governments have also rejected Chinese-made equipment designed to combat the coronavirus outbreak.

"If 2019 was the year when Europeans began having serious doubts about Beijing's geopolitical intentions, 2020 may go down in history as the moment they turned against China in defiance," Bloomberg has commented.

And just consider this upcoming drama: An overwhelming majority of those polled in a UK survey believe Britain should pull out of the 2022 Winter Olympics in Beijing in protest against the Chinese government and its human rights violations. "The whole world should pull out and boycott the games," one commentator said. Several Canadian and US politicians and international organizations have also called for a united boycott of the Beijing Olympics, with some urging the Olympic committee to revoke Beijing's right to host the games.

It would not be the first time an Olympic Games faced a walkout. The Soviet invasion of Afghanistan in 1980 prompted a US-led boycott of the summer games in Moscow that saw 66 countries stay away. In return, the Soviet Union and 17 other countries, mainly its Communist allies, boycotted the 1984 games in Los Angeles.

China skipped the 1980 Olympics but participated in the 1984 games. State-controlled Chinese media are already striking back at ideas of a 2022 boycott and warning that shunning the Beijing games would "only hurt the athletes and the population of the country".

Boycotting is an important phenomenon, as I see it, because it highlights that decoupling isn't just an issue to be viewed from a manufacturing and supply chain point of view – but in terms of consumer demand too.

True, boycotting everything produced in China is, in this age, far from easy. Impossible, some would say. People across the world may not even fully grasp just how much they consume from China – not just products labeled 'Made in China' but products stuffed with Chinese components. "They won't buy from China," a commenter wrote on social news platform Reddit. "Unless it's cheaper. Or easier to find. Or is highly recommended. Or looks nicer."

Few people know better how hard it is to stage a full Made-in-China boycott than Sara Bongiorni, the author of a book called "A year without Made in China", which was published in 2007.

The story of Bongiorni and her family's struggle to cut out everything China-made is as fascinating as it is entertaining, and perhaps better than any other report sums up the West's dependency on Chinese exports. In short, it was a struggle! Especially considering that many products filled with Chinese ingredients, like medicine, are not labeled as Chinese products. There's also no requirement to display country of origin details on non-packaged goods.

"I realized firsthand the degree to which the local shopping mall serves as an emporium of Chinese goods," Bongiorni writes in her foreword. "When friends and strangers alike ask me if life without China is possible these days, I have a ready response – one formed by a year without birthday candles, video games, and holiday decorations. Not a chance."

She doesn't blame China for American consumers being addicted to Chinese goods, which is an important point to make. We couldn't resist what China was selling, she writes. All those cheap toys, shoes and gadgets. Perhaps this is typical consumer behavior. We tell ourselves that we favor and are ready to pay a premium for products made ethically and locally, but when we make our actual purchases, all too often we go for the cheap option. And we also know, somewhere in the back of our minds, that going for the cut-rate choice is not good for our local economy; it might bring cheap and cheerful consumption to the masses, but it also undercuts products that are healthier and more sustainably or ethically produced.

Bongiorni was not the first, nor the last, to stage a China boycott. In 2004, the Wall Street Journal published a front-page story headlined 'Christmas Embargo: A Mom Bans China From Under the Tree.' While Bongiorni's efforts to avoid Chinese goods was more of an experiment, Peggy Smedley, who featured in the WSJ story, had a conviction that "China is really draining American manufacturing" and destroying American jobs. But that could change, she stressed, if American consumers made it a point to buy American-made goods. "I know that when you get on a soapbox people think you're losing it," she said. "But you really have to start somewhere."

Today, as the FTI survey shows, she's not alone on that soapbox anymore. Readiness to leave Chinese goods on the shelves might be a new trend that will actually benefit local producers and the creation of new trade partnerships. It could also, worryingly, indicate a turn toward increased protectionism and nationalism.

In the epilog of Sara Bongiorni's book, she writes that she would be reluctant to ever again stage a boycott of Chinese products, considering how energy-draining the exercise was for her family. "In some ways I'd rather not know how much harder life without Chinese goods might be a decade from now," she writes.

To consider that question, I conducted an interview with Bongiorni, who lives in New Orleans. I asked her whether more than a decade later, she still thinks it would be harder to do a Made in China boycott today.

Her answer was clear: Yes, it would. The world is even more entangled and many more products, even without Made in China labels, are likely to have Chinese components and ingredients. She's especially worried, she said, about China's chokehold over the US on medicine and healthcare products, something that's been exposed during the pandemic. She also acknowledged the ideological clash between China and Western democracies.

"Some 10-15 years ago, the greatest concern related to production moving to China was the impact on American workers, loss of jobs in small towns, and intellectual property," Bongiorni told me. "Now there's also growing concern about access to medicine and protective gear and those supply chains, as well as the political tug-of-war that's going on."

She stressed that the "hard feelings" against China in the US are not against the Chinese people in general – but the Chinese government. That's a statement I hear all the time, almost daily, when I speak with people about the clash.

Bongiorni is also concerned about how US companies and organizations play a morally compromised double-game: They say they stand for democratic values, equality and human rights – but turn a blind eye to human rights violations when it comes to their business interests in China. American consumers should be ready to reject any company connected to dishonorable behaviors, she said.

One of the most striking examples of this, and one cited by Bongiorni, relates to the National Basketball Association. The NBA has found itself in the middle of a geopolitical and ideological clash thanks to a series of embarrassing gaffes. It has reportedly turned a blind eye to abuse and neglect at its training academies in Xinjiang, a facility "located in a region notorious for the mass murder of Uighur Muslims and other ethnic minorities, compulsory political re-education, and one of the most extensive internments of civilians in concentration camps since the Holocaust", according to a WSJ op-ed headlined 'The NBA's Moral Failure in China.'

In 2019, a tweet by the Houston Rockets' general manager, Daryl Morey, declaring "Fight for Freedom. Stand with Hong Kong," awoke fury in Beijing – and the NBA quickly bowed its head and kowtowed to the Communist regime, clearly hoping to protect its personal business interests at the expense of free speech. The NBA has been repeatedly slammed for "wimping out", as Bongiorni put it to me.

"Consumers around the world can really put pressure on companies and organizations like the NBA to make the right call," she told me over a video link.

"We will see more of that. I mean, why would you give your money to a company that seemingly supports oppression of human rights?"

"You can't say you're for social justice when it comes to Black Lives Matter, but at the same time say, 'Never mind, they lock up a million Muslims in China; we're not gonna bother with that.' They will really have to make a decision."

Another US organization to come under fire for its cozy relationship with Beijing is Disney, most recently over its live-action remake of 'Mulan'. Shot in Xinjiang, the film's end-credits offer "special thanks" to eight government organizations in the province, including the public security bureau in Turpan, a city in eastern Xinjiang where several brutal internment camps have been documented. It didn't take long for #BoycottMulan to trend on Twitter – while Chinese citizens voiced their support for the movie.

Bongiorni believes many people in the US and other democratic societies would be more than happy to choose non-Chinese products if they had the option, and that companies selling products not made in China could use this as a selling point to increase sales.

"Oh, absolutely. There would be a tremendous demand for that," she said.

She also questioned whether governments and companies around the world actually have to be so afraid of China. In her view, Beijing can never be a world leader because of its political limitations.

On that question, she made reference to the Wizard of Oz, the 1939 American musical fantasy film:

"When they finally find the wizard it's just a little man behind the curtain, when everybody thought he was gonna be this big powerful person. In some ways, that's how I feel China is. Look behind the curtain and it's just an authoritarian regime. They have a huge economy, but no one is inspired by China – unless it's maybe North Korea. That's the only place where you can possibly think you're moving up if you escape to China."

In India, a countrywide "boycott China" movement has already gained steam. It's connected to the virus outbreak and a recent deadly military border clash with China, but also fueled by long-standing cranky diplomatic and cultural relationships between the two countries.

(As an aside, I'll never forget a seminar I attended in Shenzhen which had the purported aim of promoting collaboration between Chinese and Indian tech startups. A Chinese businessman slammed the idea as impossible because "you can't eat curry with chopsticks.")

The hashtags #BoycottMadeInChina, #RemoveChinaApps and #MadeinIndia have gone viral on social media, as part of nationwide calls for boycotts of Chinese products, services and companies. Billboards declaring "Boycott China" can be seen along roads and protests have been staged outside the premises of Chinese companies, including mobile phone maker Oppo, where demonstrators have burned the Chinese flag and posters of president Xi Jinping. One Indian netizen made a historical reference: "Just as India led its Freedom Struggle, the same way we consumers have to lead this struggle and free ourselves from Chinese products."

A state-of-the-nation survey found 90 percent of polled Indians said they would like China-made products to be banned in the country.

The Indian government hasn't explicitly announced a boycott, but by all accounts states and public sector companies have been asked to desist from issuing new contracts to Chinese companies, according to the BBC. The government is also urging e-commerce companies including the start-up Flipkart and Amazon India to label all products sold on their websites with country-of-origin information.

Bilateral trade between China and India, already down by 15 percent since the 2018 financial year, could now take a further hit as New Delhi mulls extra tariffs and anti-dumping duties on Chinese imports, the BBC said. Since the border clash in July 2020, diplomats have expected India to deny Huawei entry into the Indian market to build a 5G network.

Even before the White House cracked down on WeChat and TikTok, India had already banned those two apps and dozens more, citing national security concerns. Celebrities and television anchors have repeatedly advocated the deletion of Chinese apps for spreading fake news and stealing personal data. India is the world's second largest app market after China.

In a way, as some experts have noted, India may ultimately prove to be a testing lab for what the US might do if China relations continue to worsen.

Chinese state-controlled media have unexpectedly pushed back against the boycotts in India, often in pretty aggressive tones. The Global Times newspaper, one of Beijing's propaganda megaphones, said it would "be extremely dangerous for India to allow anti-China groups to stir public opinion, thus escalating tensions".

Again, boycotting Made in China is easier said than done. But the campaign is making its mark. Samsung has already increased sales of mobile phones in India on the back of anti-Chinese sentiment, jumping from a market share of 16 percent in the first quarter of 2020 to 26 percent in the second. Its main competitor, China's Xiaomi, is ironically banking on a 'Made in India' image to beat the backlash.

(As another aside, one small detail indicates that India might actually have a better chance than the US of reshoring production. You probably remember claims that Donald Trump's red "Make America Great Again" caps were actually made in China. Rumors had it that similar red caps in India with "Boycott China" were also made in China. An investigative report debunked the theory – the caps were Indian-made.)

For added irony, it may even be the case that the part of the world with the greatest public crusade against Chinese products and services is actually in China. One way to support the pro-democracy movement in Hong Kong and to protest against the communist regime in Beijing – without violating the new national security law – is to shop, eat and consume your entertainment within the so-called "yellow economic circle".

"What do you do in a non-democratic society where the government refuses to listen to you? In a money-driven city like Hong Kong, you use your wallet," an analyst at a high-end wealth management firm in Hong Kong told me.

Business in Hong Kong is today color-coded. The yellow economy has become an informal system of classifying thousands of businesses based on their support for the pro-democracy movement. It's sometimes referred to as the anti-communist economic circle. Blue, meanwhile, symbolizes support for Beijing and the Hong Kong police.

Before the national security law took effect in July 2020, yellow cafés and shops across town were usually colorfully decorated with posters and stickers supporting democracy or demanding freedom for Hong Kong. Often to be found at these places were so-called 'Lennon Walls' covered in Post-it notes inscribed with phrases such as "You Are Not Alone" and "Never Forget!" – or more offensive slogans such as "Fuck the HK police" and "HK is not China."

Now, however, such notices are considered a potential threat to national security. In fact, among the first people to be arrested under the new law was a 19-year-old boy with a sticker on his phone promoting democracy. But Hong Kong people are creative. One way around the censorship has been to still use colorful Post-it notes – but with no text. Everyone knows what they mean. Another way has been to use revolutionary slogans from Mao Zedong, such as: "Revolution Is No Crime! To Rebel Is Justified!" and "Carry the Revolution Through to the End." Quotes by Chairman Mao couldn't be deemed a threat to national security, could they?

In economic terms, the yellow circle has been instrumental in ensuring the survival of several restaurants and small shops. The owner of a small openly pro-democratic café where I often have coffee in the morning says customers come to his place for political as well as gustatory reasons. The café is listed on various popular apps and social media groups for yellow businesses. The owner tells me he tries to do most of his own shopping with yellow businesses, and shuns blue businesses like the plague.

Finding economic data on the yellow economy is not easy. But it's big enough to draw criticism from the leaders in Beijing, whose Liaison Office in Hong Kong issued a statement declaring that those who promote the yellow economic circle are "ignoring the rules of the free market." When you think about it, that's a very odd statement and makes me wonder whether the representatives for the Communist regime understand what a "free market" actually is. Choosing how you spend your money is precisely the definition of a free market. That would go without saying in most societies, but apparently not in Hong Kong.

"The yellow economy's goal long-term is about making structural changes to Hong Kong's economy," Kelvin Lam, a Democratic Party district councilor who was formerly a Greater China economist at HSBC, told Bloomberg. "We're trying to implement this yellow economy so we don't rely so much on Chinese demand and supply."

In an article published in December 2019, Simon X.H. Shen, a professor at the Chinese University of Hong Kong, estimated the market for yellow businesses could exceed HK$100 billion (US$12.9 billion).

Another way of backing the pro-democratic movement arose after media mogul Jimmy Lai, owner of the Next Digital media group and a prominent democracy campaigner, was arrested, along with several people associated with him, under the national security law, and hundreds of police stormed the editorial offices of his newspaper, Apple Daily. To show support, an army of small savers and big investors bought shares in the company – which rallied 344 percent in a few hours and by more than 1,000 percent over two days. Stock market analysts were stunned. Some called it a "protest rally". Some of my friends made some money off the surge, and pledged to spend their profits exclusively in the yellow economy.

Again, this illustrates that people have the power to use their wallets as a political tool – especially in a society where freedom of speech can no longer be taken for granted.

Meanwhile, there's also a push from company owners in Hong Kong not to manufacture products in mainland China, but to have them made in other countries in the region – or even in Hong Kong itself. Some Hong Kong high-tech firms have also been shifting away from mainland supply chains.

"This is the first time in history we can see an organized

movement within the business sector to step out and support the pro-democracy movement," Brian Fong, a university professor who founded the Hong Kong Business Association of Sustainable Economy (HKBase), told Bloomberg.

The organization acts as an informal chamber of commerce for the yellow economy and helps members to find products and suppliers in such places as Taiwan and Southeast Asia instead of mainland China.

"If we can help reduce dependence on China from 100 percent to 50 percent, then we will have larger room to support democracy," Fong said.

The same mantra could apply in any country or region where citizens and companies feel that they have to stand up for what they find important and worth fighting for.

During a jam-packed press conference, I asked Joshua Wong – perhaps the most internationally-recognized pro-democracy activist in Hong Kong – if he thought the yellow economy had the power to spread internationally and if he would encourage consumers around the world to boycott products made in China. The day before the press conference, Wong was one of several pro-democratic politicians who'd been disqualified from running for the legislative council, the city's semi-democratic parliament. Having spoken with him and some of his closest allies several times on the streets during the umbrella movement protests in

2014, and now again during the 2019-20 protests, I could tell he was seething with frustration.

Interestingly, he did not call for a full-scale boycott of Made in China. A common phrase among pro-democracy activists in Hong Kong is that their enemy isn't ordinary people in China – most of whom just want to get on with their lives like most people across the world – but the Communist regime and those who support it. For Wong, the main goal is to boycott "red capitalists", companies loyal and instrumental to Beijing.

"Encouraging consumers to boycott products supporting the Chinese government, or red capital, is the discussion of the resistance camp", he said, adding with emphasis:

"I urge the world to stand with Hong Kong. Actions speak louder than words."

BONUS CHAPTER

Here follows an abstract – the first chapter – from my last book, 'Shenzhen Superstars – How China's smartest city is challenging Silicon Valley'. As mentioned in my introduction, much has happened since it was published. We're in the middle of a burning trade war, and the sentiment toward China has turned from curiosity to suspicion. Still, both books have one thing in common: They focus on opportunities and ways forward in a fast-changing world. You'll find 'Shenzhen Superstars' on Amazon, both as an e-book and in paperback. Enjoy.

WHEN THE IPHONE HACKER CAME TO TOWN

When Silicon Valley veteran Scotty Allen first came to the southern Chinese city of Shenzhen a few years ago as part of an organized tour for American tech geeks, and witnessed the city's noisy hardware and electronics markets, its buzzing tech startup scene and countless glittering skyscrapers, his spontaneous reaction was not: "Wow, this is cool." It was: "Wow, we are fucked".

That was in 2015, and it was a visit that turned out to be a life-changing experience. He realized that something unique was happening in this Chinese city – a city that he, along with most of his colleagues and friends in the US, were not aware of. To put it starkly, he knew that China was about to outsmart the West in terms of technology.

"Coming to Shenzhen is like visiting the future. But it's this crazy Blade Runner-esque future", says Allen, his bearded, somewhat wild-looking face beaming in a broad smile. "There's this incredible energy here. There's a sort of feeling that like all boats are rising. People are just really smart and really innovative and really creative."

We meet in a coffee shop in the downtown area. It's Tuesday evening, and outside on the noisy street puddles reflect the light from small noodle bars' neon signage. Well-dressed office workers and young students hasten for the metro station, their faces illuminated by the screens on their mobile phones, to which their eyes are glued. A garbage man is swiping up electronic waste from the sidewalk, and I can see an old woman dismantling an air conditioner for scrap parts. Some buildings are modern and futuristic while others look ready to be torn down. Small hole-in-the-wall shops display everything from mobile phones and mini drones to pets and handbags. The subtropical summer heat is sticky.

Thirty-eight year old Allen is originally from south California and calls himself a software engineer by training and an entrepreneur by personality. He spent several years as a software engineer at Google, specializing in search infrastructure and user experience, then bounced around at a number of prominent startups in the Valley, including Ooyala and Shopkick. Working for these companies was amazing, he says, adding that he worked with super smart people. But it also involved "working my butt off and getting totally burned out". After starting his own company, Appmonsta – a big-data firm that provides app marketplace information – he realized he was still struggling to find his place and meaning in the corporate environment. "We were writing a whole bunch of code and sold contracts to Fortune 500 companies and did large scale enterprise sales. And I hated it", he tells me. "So I fired myself."

He ended up in Shenzhen via the above-mentioned hacker trip to China, which was organized by a friend he'd met through the Noisebridge hacker space in San Francisco. Some two dozens tech enthusiasts participated in that trip, which also took in Hong Kong, Shanghai and Beijing. In Shenzhen the group visited several open-source hardware companies (including Seeed Studio and Dangerous Prototypes) and hacker spaces (Chaihuo Makerspace and SZDIY), and they were also shown around town by local tech buffs.

What made the most profound impression on Allen was the

city's exhilaratingly buzzy, noisy Huaqiangbei electronics market. The largest hub in the world for electronic components, it offers everything from circuit boards to LED lights, drones and computer-controlled cutting machines – all at remarkably low prices. Tech Radar once called Shenzhen "the global gadget capital", and I'm pretty sure they were referring to the Mecca that is Huaqiangbei. The area is basically a one-mile strip with ten-story buildings on both sides of the boulevard filled to the brim with electrical stuff, both legal and illegal. It's any tech nerd's candy store.

Scotty Allen was sold.

"I came to Shenzhen and totally fell in love with it. When we were done in Beijing I immediately bought a train ticket back here to Shenzhen. And I've benn coming and going ever since," he says.
He admits, somewhat reluctantly, that like many other Westerners he had a prejudiced – or at least uninformed – view of China as a poor country with an economy based on low-level manufacturing and cheap piracy.

"I'm kind of ashamed to admit this, but I came in with the attitude that China is far behind the US – a place where we farm out the stuff that we don't want to do," he says. "It was an attitude of superiority. But the reality was very different. I realized there was more money here than I thought there was. It was way higher tech. The infrastructure was way better. In most ways, Shenzhen is actually a nicer city than San Francisco."

Today Allen has become a specialist on the south Chinese city's electronics-manufacturing scene – the industrial markets, factories and back alleys where the world's electronics are made. You might actually already have heard about him. Allen is that guy who built his own iPhone from the ground up by using only recycled and spare parts that he found at the local electronics markets.

The inspiration to do so came one boozy evening at a barbecue joint in the city when a friend speculated whether it might be possible. Scotty took up the challenge. Initially, he wasn't even sure whether he would be able to source all the parts. On his popular Youtube channel Strange Parts he documents scouting around dozens of small stores at the electronic markets in search of the components needed for his phone's screen, shell, battery and logic board. The video takes you from the main markets to hidden alleys, even to a cellphone repair school. The process was far from easy, and on several occasions he had to return to the same store to replace components or seek advice. But eventually, with many a teachable moment along the way, he was able to build a completely functional iPhone 6s. Allen says the phone's parts cost him about US$300. By comparison, an iPhone 6S from Apple starts at around $550.

Sitting at the café, he shows me the phone and I play around with it for a while. I can't honestly tell it's not an original. I'm far from an expert but I've tried out many iPhone and Android rip-offs in China and you can normally tell a fake one instantly. Scotty's, though, is just perfect: the screen swipes easily; apps open and close; the camera and compass work, as do all the other apps I try out. Scotty emphasizes that it's not a rip-off – it's a remake of mainly recycled parts, just like building a car from old parts from the scrap yard. The project whetted his appetite and on his Youtube channel you can watch even geekier DIY adventures from the streets of Shenzhen.

Making the iPhone was more than a fun hobby project. It was an experiment to see whether Shenzhen could deliver on its reputation as a gadget utopia. The city passed the test, and Allen does not think it would be possible to make a phone from scratch like this in any other part of the world.

"The availability in Shenzhen is phenomenal. I can walk to the markets 10 or 15 minutes from where I'm staying and find a lot of the parts I need. Anything rare that I can't find myself can be delivered to me within a day. In the States, for hobbyist level stuff it takes closer to weeks and it is many times the price.

"This is unique. I think this is one of the first places where it really feels like just about anything is possible."

Part of the equation is that Shenzhen is more than just a city. It's the heart of the Pearl River Delta, one of China's most powerful business and manufacturing clusters, and is situated right by the border to Hong Kong, one of the world's leading financial centers and still an important gateway between East and West. While the dirtiest factories have now left Shenzhen itself and the city is increasingly built on high finance, high tech and creativity, it remains surrounded by the world's most complete supply chain for hardware manufacturing.

This infrastructure has created one of the world's most powerful hubs for manufacturing smart hardware. While the US is dominant in the software field, China – and especially Shenzhen and the Pearl River Delta – has the advantage in hardware.

Numerous American and Asian entrepreneurs interviewed for this book, not to mention international venture capitalists, are clear that Shenzhen is streets ahead in a lot of areas, from robotics to self-driving cars.

For Scotty, who has spent years getting to know what makes the US' and China's main innovation hubs unique, this is strikingly obvious.

"Silicon Valley in San Francisco is no longer Silicon Valley. It's really Software Valley. I don't think there's much good hardware innovation in the Valley. Shenzhen is definitely the new Silicon Valley in terms of hardware production", he says.

Today, companies in Shenzhen already spend more on research and development than in any other city in China, and innovation-driven sectors – from ICT to biotech – make up bigger parts of its economy than anywhere else. In fact, companies in Shenzhen apply for more international patents than the whole of the United Kingdom. (We'll dive deeper into numbers later in the book.)

The city is home to some of the world's leading and most innovative technology companies, many of them firms that people in the West probably haven't heard of. Let's just look at some of the headline acts. Shenzhen has one of the world's biggest internet companies (Tencent recently surpassed Facebook in market value), the world's biggest maker of drones (Anyone flying past DJI lately? Not likely), the world's biggest maker of plug-in electric cars (Nope, it's not Tesla, it's BYD); and the world's biggest telecoms equipment company (Huawei is three times bigger than its closest rival, Sweden's Ericsson).

Oh, and did I mention where Apple has set up its latest research and development center? No prizes for guessing.

The city is also home to some of the most inspirational startup entrepreneurs I've ever met, with businesses ranging from financial, medical and education technology to wealth management and hospitality. On one occasion I got a ride in a taxi that the cabbie had turned into mobile version of 7-Eleven, selling everything from nuts and dried mango to umbrellas via QR codes and mobile payments. Many of the city's tech startups (okay, maybe not the taxi guy) already have valuations of millions of dollars, and are breaking new ground in everything from financial services, automation and robotics to artificial intelligence and virtual reality.

While there are many factors connecting Silicon Valley and Shenzhen – people are, stereotypically, young, hungry and highly educated – Scotty also sees striking differences in behavior. In the US, if you have an idea, the assumption is that you're going to use what you have available to make everything yourself. In China, people are more likely to work in a network of other people, he explains. It's all about whom you know and who has the right machines to help you with your prototype. Vertical integration, where one company can do the entire project soup to nuts, is less common here. Allen's biggest tip for people coming to Shenzhen is to be prepared to jump in with both feet and be ready to engage with the community. This is not a situation where you can show up with a design, throw it over the wall, and expect to get back a perfect production run or a perfect prototype, he says.

"Expect to go to factories to get your hands dirty. Talk with the engineers and the workers. Also, expect that things will go wrong. Manufacturing is hard. But if you approach it from the perspective of a partnership, that you're working together as a team with the factory, you can get really high results. You're going to need to put in the hours."

Even if many products are still getting designed in San Francisco, they are, for the most part, being manufactured here in Shenzhen, he says. Or, if they're not, they're still using parts coming out of Shenzhen. In hardware, at least if you need volume, it's just hard not to touch upon Shenzhen.

For Scotty Allen, however, what's important is not whether Shenzhen or Silicon Valley is ahead. It's more about both doing great, and existing in symbiosis, rather than as rivals. He no longer sees it as the US versus China, but rather a situation where all advance together, he explains. He does, however, encourage more Westerners to come to Shenzhen and experience the amazing development and opportunities in the city.

As he sips his tea, I ask Allen to explain the one thing that for him defines the city, that special detail that makes it what it is. Again, his bearded face shines up in a broad smile.

"Shenzhen has an energy of growth – the same energy I felt when I first came to Silicon Valley ten years ago," he says. "And it's not just in technology. It's this idea that whoever you are, whatever you're into, you can come to China, and especially Shenzhen, and do it!"

ACKNOWLEDGEMENTS

This book is the result of many travels in China and neighboring countries over several years, although most of the research is new. In a way, I haven't been alone in writing the book. Journalists and analysts around the world are all trying to make sense of the situation, and many new eye-opening reports flood the wires daily. By a similar token, perhaps the main challenge has been that everything right now is moving so fast – in fact, even as I type these words I'm distracted by the ping of trade war-related news notifications.

They say journalism is a rough draft of history and that the academics deal with the details later on. One thing is clear, though: the historians will be waiting a while before the drafts are done on this conflict. The battle of ideologies has only just started.

I'd like to give a massive shout-out to all friends and good people here in Hong Kong and across the world for uncompromisingly standing up for what's right and decent. Remember the words of Boris Yeltsin: "We don't appreciate what we have until it's gone. Freedom is like that. It's like air. When you have it, you don't notice it."

Please sign up for my next book at johannylander.asia.

DON'T FORGET MY FREE GIFT TO YOU

Just a friendly reminder: If you would like access to a documentary-style presentation I've made on the topic of this book, please e-mail me at theepicsplitbook@gmail.com with the subject line FREE GIFT.

This is my way of saying thanks for purchasing this book.

Printed in Great Britain
by Amazon